GOD'S WILL
FOR THE
REST OF US

FOUR PERSPECTIVES OF
A VICTORIOUS CHRISTIAN LIFE

TOM MAYHEW

Is one of my closest Friends,
An Army grunt, engineer, Pastor,
executive, Navy Captain who
deployed To Iraq with the
Marines.

GOD'S WILL
FOR THE REST OF US

Printed by CreateSpace Publishing
(www.createspace.com)

ISBN: 1439272743
ISBN-13: 9781439272749
LCCN: 2010908357

*To Kathy, my soul mate, the wisest
woman I've ever known, who showed me
God's strength-training program
through her own life.*

DISCLAIMER:

Any references contained within this book to the United States Armed Forces or any branch of the military services are my own observations and opinions. No reference or statement herein reflects any official position, stated or implied, of the U.S. Air Force, U.S. Army, U.S. Navy, U.S. Marine Corps, Department of Defense, or any other government agency.

TABLE OF CONTENTS

INTRODUCTION:
WHO ARE THE REST OF US?

You know, some people find their life's soul mate in high school and they know as teenagers what they want to be for the rest of their life. They set out on their course, stick with it, and move ahead without looking back or thinking about "what might have been."

I'm not one of them. I suppose you aren't either.

What is God's will for my life? We know this question can be asked a thousand different ways. It can apply to the next two minutes or to the rest of our lives. In my own search for God's will, I'll admit this right off the bat: I've had many arguments with God over what was, or wasn't, His will for my life. I'd plead with Him, "Why can't I have this wife, college, job, house, friend, fun, or money? Could you give me a little direction, please?"

As you'll see in the pages ahead, God patiently worked with me—just as He'll do with you. Although it took a while, He showed me that His plan was much richer—and wiser—than any I might have cooked up on my own. It was difficult and challenging, yes, but His plan made me a much stronger instrument for His purposes and put me in a much better position to receive His blessings.

You may ask, "Who are you to tell me about how to find God's will?" For starters, I earned a theology degree from an evangelical Bible college, preparing to go into the full-time ministry. Because my life wasn't following a straight line, I became interested in the subject of God's will. I've taken classes and spent many hours on mind-numbing analysis of theology, Greek grammar, historical context, church doctrine, and anything else I could find related to this topic. I have over forty books in my library on God's will and have read many of them several times. Through all this research, I believe I've found a fresh perspective on how to find and follow God's will. I hope you'll find it helpful to your own search.

After Bible college, my life took a different turn into the business world where I've spent the past twenty-five years, much of that time as a senior manager in the highly competitive computer software industry. I couldn't find much advice from my books on how to find God's will there, so I had to sign up for the "school of hard knocks." It was there I learned what God expected of me "in the world" as I went to work each day. At the same time, I've served with four branches of the military over the past three decades. In late 2006, I deployed to Iraq with the Marine Corps during what many consider the worst period of that war. These experiences forced the "head knowledge" of God's will into my heart, providing a realistic sense of what works and what doesn't.

I got married when I was thirty-six years old, well into the "confirmed bachelor for life" age bracket. For years I asked God if I'd ever find "the right one." I knew in my heart that God had someone special in mind for me. I held out for years, praying and waiting, often in deep discouragement. Kathy, my wife, turned out to be completely worth the wait. But she did not come down the road where I was looking, at all. You wouldn't believe the lessons about God's will I learned here. Kathy is my other half, my soul mate, my partner in the adventures of life and in the missions God has placed before us. He obviously knew what He was doing.

For whatever reason, He made me wait a long time and go through some painful experiences before I met Kathy. Similarly, I went through some painful jobs to learn how to find God's will for that big part of my life that was taking place outside the church building. I started out as a cook at McDonald's. I then joined the army and flew helicopters for three years. Later, I taught math and physical education in a Christian high school—and worked as a janitor. I spent ten years in college, earning three degrees in completely different fields: theology, electrical engineering, and corporate finance.

Years later, I worked as a radar engineer and then moved into the computer software industry as a project manager leading engineering, sales, and marketing strategy teams. I spent fourteen years at one of the most ruthlessly competitive powerhouse software companies on the planet. I participated in a couple of Silicon Valley Internet startups, managed several global business initiatives, and served on several industry and non-profit boards of directors.

You may be thinking, *Wow, did this guy have a clue what he wanted to be when he grew up?*

No.

More often than I care to admit, I had no clear sense at all whether I was in the right place or if I had missed something along the way. Few of the books I'd read about God's will got to the heart of my questions about how to know if I were making the right decisions. I'd often get conflicting advice from well-meaning friends, family, and church leaders. More than once, the major life decisions I made did not look wise to others. Of course, all kinds of fear, guilt, and second-guessing cropped up along the way like part of some package deal. It was incredibly difficult and frustrating to try and follow God's leading. But I found a way and I believe it can be of great help to "the rest of us" who are seeking God's will. That's why I wrote this book.

In the chapters ahead, I want to show you some promises God has made to Christians who do not work in a full-time ministry. I would like to show you the Bible's answers to questions such as these:

How can a person be sure he or she is on the right track with God?

How does God actually lead us toward His plan and His blessings?

How can a Christian succeed in the business world and still keep his or her morality—and sanity?

How does a Christian make the right decisions when there is so much temptation to do wrong?

If the path we're on is difficult, is it the wrong one?

How can we establish a close, intimate relationship with God that works all the time, inside and outside the church building?

How can I be sure God is leading me when my world is falling apart?

The answers to these questions not only help God's people find inner peace and spiritual strength, they open up tremendous opportunities to help those around us who are in need. And they open the floodgates of heaven for us to receive the blessings of God. Here's an obvious statement: Since we are still alive, God is not yet through with us. Even if you or I were lying in a bed with advanced Alzheimer's disease, oblivious to the world around us, we would still be God's instrument to work His will. Until we draw our last breath, He has a plan for our lives and missions for us to fulfill. Philippians 1:6 says, "Being confident of this, that he who began a good work in you will carry it on to completion until the day of Christ Jesus." Young person or old, brand-new Christian or war-weary believer of many years, this book is meant for you. God knows about your situation and wants you to know He cares deeply where you are headed.

God's will is not just about us. It's about the effect we have on others. Going back to the person with Alzheimer's disease, he or she has a profound influence on those nearby, providing an opportunity for them to respond to a mission sent from God and as sacred as any full-time ministry. We'll see why God's will is a difficult and challenging training program that brings about great reward. It's a vicious fight against a brutal and determined enemy. It is a beautiful relationship with the Creator of the entire universe. It is preparation for an even greater life with Him in eternity. And it is the promise of great reward to those who endure to the end and stay faithful to the One who gave it all for us on the cross.

God promises He will bless those who follow Him. If we let Him, He will lead us into a relationship with Him that trains and strengthens us to be victorious, champion Christians. As we gain maturity and strength in our faith we can, as Hebrews 12:10 says, "partake in His holiness" and fulfill the challenging missions He's chosen specifically for us. In John 16:33, Jesus said, "In this world you will have tribulation, but be of good cheer, I have overcome the world."

PART I:
QUESTIONS

WHY DID THIS HAPPEN?

Years ago, a Baptist missionary left the mission field in discouragement and became a police officer in a large city in the southern United States. One day, while patrolling in an inner-city neighborhood, he got into a struggle with an angry, armed young man. The former-missionary-turned-policeman tried to calm down this individual and get him to give up the weapon.

A small group of people had gathered nearby to watch this scene unfold. Angry at their situation in life, angry at the police, and angry at the world, these people yelled at the young man and encouraged him to shoot the cop. He did, and the former-missionary-turned-police-officer died. This senseless murder set off a string of protests in the city. Weeks later, the incident was all but forgotten by everyone except the policeman's family and friends, and the murderer who was now in jail.

I first heard this story over twenty-five years ago and have thought about it many times since then. To me, it provokes a lot of questions about God's will. Many Christians who heard the story at the time believed that the former-missionary-turned-police-officer had run from God and was now being called home early because of his disobedience to "God's will for his life."

What actually happened that day? Are we sure this Christian missionary-turned-police officer was out of God's will? What if he were still following Him, just not in the full-time ministry? What if he was God's chosen instrument at that tragic time and place to intervene in the lives of those who were there? What if this missionary-turned-cop, in his moment of mortal danger, was God's special agent, His witness to those who were yelling at the young man to shoot him? Could he have been the "chosen knight" standing in the gap between the powers of darkness and light, between the eternal domains of Satan and Jesus Christ, battling for the souls of those who were there?

Whatever took place that day in the ongoing battle between good and evil, it would appear from an earthly perspective that evil won. But we can say with certainty that God's will was accomplished and this was part of His sovereign, ultimate plan. I believe the Bible is God's Word, and it says nothing takes Him by surprise. He sees the beginning from the end. This is announced powerfully in Isaiah 46:9–11:

Remember the former things, those of long ago; I am God, and there is no other;

I am God, and there is none like me. I make known the end from the beginning, from ancient times, what is still to come. I say: My purpose will stand, and I will do all that I please.

From the east I summon a bird of prey; from a far-off land, a man to fulfill my purpose. What I have said, that will I bring about; what I have planned, that will I do.

Proverbs 8:15 and 21:1 tell us that God raises up good and evil kings for His own purposes. The Old Testament prophet Isaiah relates how God "summoned" Cyrus, the first king of Persia, by name, over a century and a half before he actually came to power. Jesus Christ told His disciples that a sparrow doesn't fall to the earth without God knowing about it. The Old Testament book of Job is a front-row-seat view of a godly man who unknowingly served as an object lesson in a cosmic-scale, spiritual confrontation between God and Satan! It also shows us how Job's wife and his three supposedly well-meaning friends added to his suffering when they offered their unsolicited and, it turns out, uninformed opinions on his sin, guilt, and judgment.

Romans 8:28 is a familiar and timeless verse of comfort to Christians. You can probably say it by heart: "All things work together for good to those who love

God, who are called according to His purpose." God's ultimate plans are not derailed by our sins or the decisions we make. You and I may not understand why the missionary-turned-police-officer was killed on an ugly street in a large southern city. God does. For reasons we cannot yet fathom, it fulfilled part of His ultimate and eternal purpose. We won't know until the next life what impact the police officer's actions had in the spiritual world we can't see, or whether they eventually resulted in the redemption of many people.

Closer to home, it's incredibly difficult to grasp God's ultimate purpose when you're standing over the fresh grave of a suddenly departed loved one. I've seen friends of mine struggle to believe He's in control of anything when they're looking through the thick windowpane of the intensive care ward, watching their sick newborn child fight for life. When trials, temptations, disappointments, and financial difficulties hit us like a violent tornado, it's hard to see how—or where—God is leading us. All too often, we blame Him for what is happening.

In John 9:1–3, when Jesus and His disciples walked by a person who was born blind, they asked Him whether this individual or his parents had sinned to bring on such a tragic judgment. Jesus said, "Neither, this has happened so that the work of God could be displayed and glorified in his life." God's eternal purposes define His ultimate will, and we can't know those purposes here on earth unless He chooses to reveal them to us.

On the other hand, the Bible explicitly says that every one of us will one day give a detailed account of our lives to Him. Jesus Christ said in Matthew 12:36 (KJV), "But I say unto you, that every idle word that men shall speak, they shall give account thereof in the day of judgment." The angry young man who pulled the trigger and committed murder in that southern city, the angry people who encouraged him to do so, the former-missionary-turned-police-officer, and you and I: each of us has a destiny before God based on the decisions we've made in our lives.

It may seem difficult to reconcile these two different aspects of God's will: His ultimate plan and our daily decisions. Of course, our most important decision is whether we accept Jesus Christ as our Lord and Savior. Once we do, we embark on a life of stewardship before Him to accomplish the missions He's prepared for us. God knows the full effects and consequences of our decisions, even if we don't. He chooses, according to His eternal purposes, to reward us accordingly.

And He does have ways of letting us know what He wants.

WHY THE STRUGGLE?

I took another look at the alarm clock. Two o'clock in the morning and I was wide awake. An hour had passed since I had last glanced over there, and still no answer. I was agonizing over a decision I'd made, prayerfully, nine years before. It now looked like it had led to a dead end and a complete waste of my time. You see, when I was in high school, my dream was to attend college at the United States Air Force Academy and become an Air Force officer. I'd worked hard in school, making good grades and staying out of trouble, to be accepted into the Academy. When I graduated from high school, I realized my dream and was admitted to the Academy as a cadet. At the beginning of my senior year in high school, however, I began to feel that God had "called me to preach." I surrendered my life to serve Him in "full-time service," and decided to give up my dream of being an Air Force officer. I left the Academy to go into the ministry.

My father, who was not a born-again Christian, was firmly against this decision and refused to help me with tuition for Bible college. I was working at a fast-food restaurant and couldn't afford it on my own, so I ended up taking a significant detour to pay for college by enlisting in the army. You'll hear more about those times later. After three years in the army, four years at Bible college and two years as a Christian high school teacher, here I was, wondering why God was now clearly closing the door on my involvement in the full-time ministry. I had given Him my life and my dreams. In response, I was getting an unmistakable set of signals that He wasn't going to bless this path if I continued on it.

Praying, wrestling at two o'clock in the morning, I said to Him, "Lord, what did I do wrong? I've spent the past nine years trying to follow your will. What do I do now?"

No doubt you've had a similar experience, wrestling with God over a sick child, a wayward teenager, an abusive spouse or parent, a betraying friend, a tough decision, the loss of a job, or the grieving loss of a close loved one. It's not a fun place to be. Lying awake in the middle of the night, we ask God why and plead with Him to reveal what comes next.

Most of us Christians want to know His will, so why must this whole exercise be so difficult? Why doesn't God give us clear and simple directions on the decisions we have to make, especially when it seems so easy to go off track and miss His will? Why doesn't He just tell us what He wants us to do?

John MacArthur, in his little book *Found: God's Will*, compared the search for God's will to a big, cosmic Easter egg hunt with all of us wandering around, like little kids, looking for a hidden golden egg. Of course, you and I know people who have been certain from the time they were tiny babies what God wanted them to do with their lives. I remember a business school classmate who interviewed for a job with a major Wall Street investment firm. Since he was a little boy, he told the interviewer, he had wanted to be an equities research analyst.

Right.

I didn't even know what an equities research analyst was until he told me. Even though he sounded quite sure of the job he wanted, I'd find it hard to believe that this individual, and others like him, did not at some point wrestle with God over other decisions and circumstances they face. It is inescapable, isn't it? You may recall the Old Testament story of Jacob wrestling with God in the middle of the night, in the desert, in the midst of a personal crisis. Genesis 32:24–32 tells the story of Jacob wrestling a man all night long. When morning came, the man told Jacob to let him go. Jacob refused, saying, "I will not let you go until you bless me." The man turned out to be God Himself. The blessing Jacob received was the new name Israel, meaning "prince of God."

His name change set in motion a whole series of events that forever changed Jacob's and his children's destiny.

Now, why would God wrestle with Jacob? Why would God allow Jacob to struggle with Him, especially when, in Genesis 28:15, He told Jacob, "I am with you and will watch over you wherever you go, and I will bring you back to this land. I will not leave you until I have done what I have promised you." Most Bible commentators think, even though Jacob heard His promise, he still didn't believe it. God wrestled with him to make him stronger in his faith, to trust in the Lord and not in his own strength, so he would *believe*.

Here is an important principle for "the rest of us": God conditions us to receive His promises and the missions He's planned for us. Through the years, I have learned that when God doesn't tell us what to do, He's telling us something else: to trust Him, to grow stronger by waiting on Him, and to endure. God is telling us He wants us to experience firsthand His promise that He'll never leave or forsake us. Sometimes we have to hold our breath and take the first step through an open door into the unknown. Sometimes we have to find and crawl through an open window when all the doors are closed and locked. Sometimes we have to grab hold of God and hang on until He carries us across a wide, open abyss to the other side.

God may lead us to make decisions that bring a lot of second-guessing from others we know and respect. When I enrolled in engineering school after my nine-year detour, several church leaders told me I was turning my back on God's call to the ministry for my own selfish desires. They told me I was going for the money and prestige of a corporate career, abandoning my fellow Christian laborers who were selflessly toiling away in the full-time ministry. "Demas has forsaken me, having loved this present world," several of them said, quoting 2 Timothy 4:10.

Why would they do that? Who knows? For some, it was likely because they thought I would quit when times got tough. Others probably thought I'd do something stupid and give Christianity a bad name. Years later, their real motivation became clear. Many of them wanted me to work for them in their own ministry and help meet their own needs. Whatever they thought, they couldn't fully appreciate my personal agony in those two o'clock in the morning wrestling matches with God as I begged Him to show me His will. They weren't there when I told God I was willing to do whatever He wanted, even if I hated it, even if I believed with all my heart I should be doing something else.

Neither were they aware of the simple question God had clearly impressed on my heart:

Are you following them or are you following Me?

Take a closer look. This is a much harder question than it seems. I believe our truthful answer will determine whether we receive the blessings of God during and at the end of our life's journey or get cheated out of them. We may agree that most Christians want to know how to live a life that pleases God and matters to Him. Because the age-old question "What is God's will for my life?" has no easy or straightforward answer, many people quit or settle for less before they find out. They may take the easier path and follow someone else's guidance instead of God's. As well see in more detail later, we must be careful of this. Each of us has a responsibility to find and follow God's will for our own lives.

Others fall into a deception of Satan and chase after a false god, cheating themselves out of their reward. Many people will not accept God's answer because it does not meet their own expectations or is too far outside their comfort zone. They think God's answer is a step down, or He might actually give them something to do that they would hate. They don't want to be second-guessed by people they respect or admire. They feel safe where they are and become afraid to step out in faith to grab the prize God has put before them.

What happens if we give our lives completely to God? What will He do in response? Will He ask us to sell everything we own and move to some harsh, remote place to be a missionary? Will He make us give up our dreams and settle for something we think is second-best? Will He sentence us to a boring life?

No, we'll see it is not God's will to torture or punish us. His will is to train us, strengthen us, use us, and bless us in ways we can't even imagine. He has far too much invested in us and has made each of us unique for His own purposes. He won't waste our lives, unless we insist on wasting them ourselves.

Do you know God actually tests us to see how badly we want to follow Him? Jacob was blessed because he prevailed in his wrestling match with God. Did he beat Him? Not a chance. No, he held on until God said, "Okay, Jacob, time's up. You've shown me you're serious. Let go and I'll bless you." God allows these struggles so we will learn to hold on until He says, "Let go and I'll bless you!"

Jeremiah 29:11–13 is a passage many Christians claim as one of God's promises to provide specific guidance and direction in our lives:

> For I know the plans I have for you, declares the Lord, plans to prosper you and not to harm you, plans to give you hope and a future.
>
> Then you will call upon me and come and pray to me, and I will listen to you.
>
> You will seek me and find me when you seek me with all your heart.

Jeremiah was quoting God's words to the Jews before He sent them off to captivity in Babylon. He sentenced them to seventy years in a foreign land because of the sins they and their parents had committed. Even in judgment, God offered hope and blessing to His people. As Christians living in the church age, your sins and mine have been judged on the cross. Given this, how much more does God want to bless us? If our heart's desire is to follow the Lord, shouldn't we be willing to give up whatever is in our own lives to seek Him with all our heart? After all, as Christians, our lives belong to Him and are His to use for His own purposes. As we'll see in the pages ahead, this is what God wants from us.

GOD'S WILL BY TRIAL AND ERROR

In the first decade of the twenty-first century, many news commentators and journalists have observed that Western society is entering a "post-Christian" era. They see the diminishing influence of Christianity on our culture compared to twenty-five or fifty years ago. Surveys taken in the past ten years point to a decline in church attendance, while more and more people—even those who attend evangelical churches—increasingly identify themselves as "spiritual" rather than Christian. At the same time, Christians and non-Christians sense that history is racing to some kind of climax with the souls of humankind hanging in the balance. If we truly believe God uses His church to influence the world for His good, then the stakes are higher than ever to get it right when it comes to understanding and following His will.

Using the words of several popular books on God's will, most Christians are looking for a life of purpose, rewards, and blessings in our attempts to follow His direction for our lives. After reading all of those books in my library about God's will, I've often wondered why so much of the existing discussion is focused on life inside the church. Why is all the attention given to those few who work in the full-time ministry? I think the answer is simple. Most books on God's will are written by pastors trying to help other Christians find their way. These ministers write from their own experience and perspective, which seldom contains firsthand knowledge of life out there in "the world." Sure, their books will discuss how to approach a big life decision such as whom to marry or which college to attend, but the examples they provide often come from their counseling sessions with others.

Unfortunately for the rest of us, most of these books mention a corporate or secular work-life only in passing. As a result, many of us are left wondering whether we have missed God's "perfect" will for our lives through sin, neglect, or even our own cluelessness. How can we ever feel like we are honoring God with the non-church activities that take up most of our time? One popular book on God's will says our primary purpose in life is to get saved. Once this occurs, the well-known pastor-author goes on to say, our new primary purpose is to get involved in a church. End of discussion. Precious little is said about the time we spend outside the church building.

Is this what God had in mind for us? How can we learn to more effectively be God's chosen instruments of light in dark places, executing His mission to help those hurting and trapped people we meet in our jobs, schools, or neighborhoods? How can we become victorious Christians who understand why we're doing what we do and how to make wise decisions that honor the Lord? Because there's so little coherent guidance on God's will for our lives when we're not in church, many Christians instead rely on mystical or haphazard methods to find God's will. They never take the time to find out what absolute riches and blessings He's promised us, or where to find them in God's Word, and therefore suffer the consequences.

Most books on God's will provide sound, basic advice that goes like this: read the Bible, pray, seek wise and godly counsel, and follow the promptings of the Holy Spirit as we search for His direction in our lives. Yes, that's all true. It sounds easy enough, but for most of us it's painfully clear that the wheels have come off somewhere in the process. Our search for God's will is anything but easy and certainly is not as straightforward as following a simple formula. I don't know about you, but I've seen Christians use some pretty crazy ways to find God's will. Gary Friesen, in his book *Decision-Making and the Will of God*, wrote several chapters showing how out of hand this "mystical" approach can get, yet many Christians refuse to consider any other way.

For example, you've probably heard this one: open the Bible with your eyes closed, and put your finger on a random verse to help you make some decision. "Judas went out and hanged himself." Then another: "Go and do likewise." Gideon, in the Old Testament book of Judges, asked God to make some sheep wool wet and the surrounding ground dry so he'd be sure he was making the right decision. God did so. The next night, Gideon said, "Okay, God, now do it in reverse. Make the wool dry and the ground wet." God came through again, and Gideon finally got up and followed God's instructions. I know Christians who have run with Gideon's story and made major life decisions based on whether chocolate milk was being served in the school cafeteria on a particular day.

Other Christians believe they are too sinful to understand God's intentions. They'll consider their personal desires and do the precise opposite. I've heard this one from the pulpit: *If it's something I want, it must be against God's will. I'll do what makes me miserable.* God promised us wisdom and strength if we follow Him, not a simple recipe for mindlessly turning against our own desires and calling it His will.

Others get into a praying marathon, and the first thing they see after they're done is the sign of what God wants them to do. A few years before I met Kathy, I was praying for God to show me whether a certain young woman I was seeing might be "the one." I was driving along Interstate 25 in New Mexico, on my way to visit my good buddy Jeff, and was praying intensely about this woman. *"God, give me a sign that she's the one."*

Minutes later, a white mini-van passed me. The letters on the car's license plate were the same as her initials, and the dealer frame around the license plate was from a town matching her last name. *Okay, God, this is good enough for me! You're telling me I should marry her! Thank you! Praise your Name!* So I started chasing after my soon-to-be mate with serious determination. When she dumped me like last week's trash, I was back in front of God, beseeching Him, "O God of Abraham, Isaac and Jacob, thou who guides the hearts of all fair maidens, how could I have been so wrong? I saw the license plate! You showed me!"

Silence.

Maybe we humans are hardwired to think we need a bright shining light to show us the way. We look for an "aha" moment when God lays out the whole plan for our life. When we get up off our knees from the breakthrough prayer session, we expect to know what we're supposed to do from then on. Too often we think God's "perfect" will should be smooth sailing, free from difficulty with no margin of error. If we're following God's will, isn't our life supposed to be easy, or at least *easier*? If things aren't going our way, is it a sign that we're doing something wrong? When we find ourselves hitting roadblock after roadblock, should we take the hint, turn around, and try another road?

Proverbs 20:24 says, "How can we understand the road we travel? It is the Lord who directs our steps."

It took a while, but I finally figured out why God was silent after I chased this woman with what I thought was a sure sign of His will and it turned out so badly. God's same quiet but piercing question of several years earlier came back to me:

Are you following her or are you following Me?

God, in His silence, led me back to His Word to see why this relationship was doomed to failure. He also revealed a few things I needed to work on in my own life. Eventually I realized I didn't need some sign, which Satan could easily conjure up as well, when the guiding directions are clearly contained in His Word. A few years later I met Kathy, and have thanked Him ever since for making me wait for her.

Now, this doesn't mean God no longer gives signs or miracles. Sometimes He does, but only when they suit His purposes. I've seen God work out some amazing, split-second circumstances to lead me into new missions and opportunities—or to keep me out of trouble. More importantly, God has given clear directions in His Word to approach life's decisions. When we stray from them, we provide Satan an opportunity to deceive us and lead us off track.

We'll explore in later chapters why God purposely makes our search for His will difficult and challenging. It's not because He's mad at us or doesn't like us. It's not because He's mean or balancing His books based on the good or bad things we do each day. And despite what many people think, it's especially not because He is completely disengaged from what we humans do each day. No, God has much more at stake with us than to cast us adrift to chart the course of our lives alone.

As hard as it may be to see at times, He does it out of love. It goes back to how God fulfills His ultimate plan regardless of our decisions, yet at the same time holds us accountable for those decisions. He sees the beginning from the end, and knows at each moment what we're facing in our lives. Even if we're in the middle of the biggest train wreck of our life, God can clean us up and put us back on track. If you or I knew God's plan for our entire life right now, we'd probably take credit for it ourselves rather than give the glory to Him. We'd most likely pass up the lessons and experiences through which He wants to take us in order to strengthen us and prepare us for the prize. We'd almost certainly go for the shortcut, missing God's blessings as He uses our lives to influence and affect others in their own times of need.

IS THERE A "CENTER" OF GOD'S WILL?

Not too long ago, I had lunch with an old friend who attended Bible college with me. He was telling me about his life's journey in the many years since I'd last seen him: he'd married early, started a business and lost it; he'd gotten a divorce when his wife left him for another man. He ended up going to a different college and became a high school teacher and coach, marrying again and raising a family. During his difficult divorce, he sought the advice of a well-known and respected Christian minister and author. The minister's response, he told me, went something like this: "There is a small circle called the center of God's 'perfect will,' and there's a bigger circle of God's 'permissive will' around that."

"Unfortunately, son," the respected minister continued, "You have missed the perfect center and are going to have to settle for a life in the bigger circle." In essence, my friend got stuck with the consolation prize because of something his ex-wife did.

Where is the sovereignty of God in that? How comforting is this answer, coming from "the God of all comfort?" If I commit some big sin, does it mean I can never get back into the center of God's will? What if I took the wrong job, went to the wrong college, or got mixed up with the wrong group of people? What if I was supposed to marry a different woman, but she ran off with someone else? Does this mean I'm stuck with the consolation prize for the rest of my life?

I've heard many sermons on Romans 12:2, where preachers make elaborate distinctions among God's "good," "acceptable," and "perfect" will. It's as if there are three different and concentric circles forming some kind of bull's-eye around His plan for our lives. No, the original Greek words are adjectives, not nouns. They describe *what God's will is*, not three separate rings around a bull's-eye. Had the well-known minister known this simple truth when he talked to my friend so many years ago, he might have helped him avoid a lot of pointless grief and second-guessing after those challenges came his way.

Gary Friesen's book explains why the bull's-eye approach lacks a Scriptural basis. I'd like to add one more idea to his analysis. Let's imagine for a moment the "center of God's will" concept is true. How many of us could say we're in the exact center of His will; we've never gone off course and are living the ideal, error-free life God planned for us before the foundation of the world? Apparently, it would mean God Himself is settling for second best, because, believe me, I can count on one hand the number of adult Christians I know who have not made a major mistake in their life in disobedience to God. One could argue that those people messed up by being too conservative and timid, by not grabbing hold in faith of the opportunity God placed before them even when others thought it was a bad idea. They played it safe and may never know until they get to heaven what they passed up in this life.

Looking through the Bible, especially in the Psalms and the books of Proverbs and Ecclesiastes, we see precious few comments about "the fish that got away" or "what might have been," those lost opportunities due to a missed bull's-eye. Instead, we see a focus on what we can and should be doing now—and from now on—embodied in impassioned appeals like David's prayer in Psalm 86:11:

> *Teach me your way, O Lord, and I will walk in your truth; give me an undivided heart, that I may fear your name.*

It's my intent to show that victorious, champion-level Christianity is not about sitting quietly in church like a bunch of obedient little boys and girls, avoiding mistakes. The Christian life, one lived with total abandon to God's leading, is meant to be a series of special operations missions deep into enemy territory to take out high-value targets and rescue hostages. God wants us to follow Him up some treacherous paths so we can view the surrounding terrain from breathtaking mountaintop vistas, partaking in His holiness and enjoying the view He enjoys.

Hannah Hurnard wrote a great little book called *Hinds Feet on High Places* describing the courage and stamina it takes to follow God out of the comfortable valley and up the difficult paths to the mountaintop. The Bible challenges us to step out by faith in obedience to God, to do bold things for Him, and to believe He will lead us, provide for us, and bless us. How can we possibly meet His challenge if we think we have to settle for second best—or worse—for the rest of our lives, should we make a mistake?

Another thing to keep in mind: God is never taken by surprise by what we do. Imagine the Almighty God of the Entire Universe, who sees the beginning from the end, saying, "Oh, my, I had such big plans for Tom, but, well, he's gone off and done this crazy thing, so now I can't use him. What am I going to do? It looks like I'm going to have to cook up a Plan B."

Take a look at 2 Samuel 22:21–24, where David, the King of Israel, says:

> *The Lord has dealt with me according to my righteousness; according to the cleanness of my hands he has rewarded me.*

> *For I have kept the ways of the Lord; I have not done evil by turning from my God. All his laws are before me; I have not turned away from his decrees.*

> *I have been blameless before him and have kept myself from sin.*

Do you know this little speech took place after David committed sexual sin with Bathsheba, had her husband killed to cover his tracks, and lost his two sons, Amnon and Absalom, as a result of his disobedience? How could David say he was blameless before God and kept himself from sin?

Even though he committed these heavy-duty sins and paid dearly for the consequences, I believe David could say this because he repented. In Psalm 51, he admitted his sin before God and asked God to create a clean heart within him. He got back on his feet and kept following the Lord. He remained faithful to God's Old Testament laws, went to the priest in the Temple, and offered an innocent animal sacrifice so his sin would be covered and forgiven. Those Old Testament animal sacrifices, according to Colossians 2:14, foreshadowed the ultimate sacrifice of Jesus Christ on the cross, blotting out your sins and mine for all time through the cleansing power of His shed blood.

Even though he paid for the consequences of his sins, David did not disqualify himself by turning from God to follow false gods, idols, like his son Solomon did. The Bible describes in 1 Kings 11:9–10 what happened to Solomon:

> The Lord became angry with Solomon because his heart had turned away from the Lord, the God of Israel, who had appeared to him twice.
>
> Although he had forbidden Solomon to follow other gods, Solomon did not keep the Lord's command.

God made Solomon the wisest—and richest—man who ever lived. Unfortunately, Solomon didn't persevere, or endure, with the Lord. Instead, he chose to give up the greater blessing to follow the pagan gods of his many wives. Continuing in 1 Kings 11:11–13, we see the judgment God placed on the kingdom of Israel because of Solomon's disobedience:

> So the Lord said to Solomon, "Since this is your attitude and you have not kept my covenant and my decrees, which I commanded you, I will most certainly tear the kingdom away from you and give it to one of your subordinates.

"Nevertheless, for the sake of David your father, I will not do it during your lifetime. I will tear it out of the hand of your son.

"Yet I will not tear the whole kingdom from him, but will give him one tribe for the sake of David my servant and for the sake of Jerusalem, which I have chosen."

Had Solomon repented of his idolatry, given up the false gods and returned to worship the Lord God of Israel, God would have used him again and bestowed blessings on him. Notice that in the middle of this judgment God still gave Solomon a blessing because of his father David's enduring faithfulness.

Matthew 21:28–32 tells a story about two sons who were asked to work in a field. One said he wouldn't go but changed his mind and went. The other said he'd go but didn't. Jesus asked, "Which one did the will of the father?" Obviously, it was the one who changed his mind, repented, and went back to do the work. The point is this: even though our sin and bad decisions will bring scars and consequences, they do not permanently condemn us to a second-place standing with God. A Christian who repents and follows God in obedience will receive His blessings and a series of missions uniquely and specifically tailored to him or her. Moses, in Numbers 20:12, was not allowed to go into the Promised Land because he struck a rock when God told him to speak to it. Later, in Matthew 17:1–8, Moses appeared on the Mount of Transfiguration with the glorified Jesus Christ. How much more in "the center of God's will" can you be?

As I continued my lunch conversation with my Bible college friend, I noticed he now has a strong desire to help divorced people recover and find purpose in their lives after losing their marriages. I asked him if he would be so sensitive to the needs of divorced people today and so passionate about how to maintain a godly marriage had he not been divorced himself. He said no, probably not. My friend is a high-school coach, not a full-time church minister. But God regularly brings people, often the parents of his student athletes, with broken or breaking marriages, into his life. He's given the opportunity to point them to Jesus Christ and help them heal or, if it's soon enough, help repair and restore their marriages. Many of these people would never set foot in a church building. God used a set of difficult circumstances to train and insert His special agent, and my old friend, into this place where the need exists.

HOW DO WE FIT INTO GOD'S ULTIMATE PLAN?

Do you know God revealed the details of His ultimate plan for the New Testament church to a group of Gentile construction workers? Paul wrote the book of Ephesians to working people like you and me who were trying to make a decent living in a culture that did not worship the God of the Bible. Like us, they struggled with knowing His will in the midst of a lot of conflicting church teaching, cultural opinions, and well-meaning advice. Paul wrote his letter from a Roman jail cell to this group of Gentile Christian craftsmen and trade workers who felt betrayed and cast adrift in their beliefs.

Acts 19 tells the background story of Paul's ministry in Ephesus, a big city and cosmopolitan cultural center of Asia, now part of present-day Turkey. Paul did such miracles in the city that everyone in the entire region of Asia knew about them (Acts 19:10). His messages and the miracles he performed influenced many people to come to Christ, including those who made their living off the huge temple of the pagan goddess Artemis, or Diana, in the King James Version (KJV). Some of these people even burned the books they used for practicing occult magic and witchcraft. Needless to say, this didn't go over too well with those who continued to make their living off the pagan temple.

Another group of craftsmen started a near riot in opposition to Paul's evangelistic effect on their city and their livelihood. The Jews from Ephesus and broader Asia, no friends of Paul's, ended up having him arrested by the Romans when he later traveled to Jerusalem. The story of Paul's arrest, incarceration, and trial at the hands of the Romans begins in Acts Chapter 21 and continues to the end of that book. Paul traveled to Rome to appeal to Caesar and defend himself against the charges brought against him by the Jews from Asia. Most church historians believe Paul eventually died in the Roman jail.

Can you imagine being among those Gentile trade workers from Ephesus who gave up their livelihood to follow Jesus Christ? They found themselves questioning whether they had done the right thing in following this revolutionary new message. Paul wrote the first three chapters of Ephesians to remind these Gentile Christian craftsmen and trade workers that none of this had taken God by surprise. He reminded them of the incredible promises being realized through Jesus Christ. He told them Christ had announced His victory in the heavenly realms (to any and all pagan deities the trade workers might be afraid of having offended), and is now building His church with Jewish and Gentile believers together.

Do a study of Ephesians and you'll notice Paul used a lot of construction terminology in this letter. He talked about a building precisely fitted together, made of us Christians who are God's workmanship (or end product), built on a foundation of the apostles and prophets with Christ as the cornerstone. He also said "the middle wall of partition," a reference to the part of the Temple that symbolized the divide between God and His people, has been broken down. As a result, all believers in Jesus Christ, Jews and Gentiles alike, can now boldly approach God's throne through the sacrifice of His son on the cross.

What did Paul focus on next?

Think of all the things he could have said at this point:

> *Grab your weapons, rise up, overthrow the Roman government, and get me out of this jail!*

> *Read a career planning book, take a personality test, and enroll in a seminar to find the occupation God wants you to pursue.*

> *Go back to your jobs in the Temple of Artemis and turn that huge building into a nice sanctuary for the Grace Fellowship Church of Ephesus.*

Stay inside the church and wait for further instructions.

Sell everything you have and give it to the poor!

No, Paul didn't say any of that. Instead, in Ephesians 4:1, he called himself the *prisoner of the Lord.* Think about what this communicated to his audience: he was not the prisoner of the Romans, but of Jesus Christ Himself. Who has the ultimate authority and power over us? It is not the Romans, not Satan, not our government, not our employer, not even our family, but Jesus Christ. The second half of this verse has confused many Christians seeking God's will, "I urge you to live a life worthy of the calling you have received." The KJV says, "Walk worthy of the vocation wherewith ye are called." Many preachers have used this verse to suggest they are "called" to a certain church, and must stay in it until God calls them to some other place. I have rarely heard anyone describe my job in the software business this way. Was I "called" to leave Company A to work for its major competitor, Company B? Are you "called" to be a hairdresser or a race-car driver? Romans 11:25 is another verse often used to distinguish this view of the ministry from an ordinary job: "For God's gifts and his call are irrevocable." If this minister leaves the church and goes somewhere else, it's due to this mystical conversation he has had with God, one rarely mentioned when you or I talk about changing jobs!

Unfortunately, this idea of a calling has led to serious heartache among Christians who wonder if they can change directions without running afoul of God's will. The notion of having a mystical call for a particular job leads to many of the same problems as the "center of God's will is a bull's-eye" view-point. I knew several people from my Bible college days who felt called to go to a certain church or mission field, but could not explain why. Sadly, when the church or mission field didn't work out, these people were saddled with major guilt and disappointment. In their minds, their inability to live up to "the call" made them failures as Christians. Some of them, in their discour-agement, quit following the Lord altogether.

So, what is this calling? What do these verses mean? Am I called to be a preacher or a software sales manager? Am I called to live in California or Texas—or China? Looking at the context of the first three chapters of Ephesians, Paul was talking about something entirely different. Our calling is to be fellow-citizens, Jewish and Gentile believers together in this new entity called the *ekklesia*, the church, which God is building with His own hands. The calling is God's personal invitation to approach Him boldly and with confidence (Ephesians 2:11–22, 3:12) as fellow-citizens in His household.

We members of the twenty-first century church may not fully appreciate the big divide between Jewish and Gentile Christians in those days. One Bible commentator said the Greek word *axios*, translated in Ephesians 4:1 as "worthy" actually means "equal weight." Paul encouraged the Gentile Christians in Ephesus literally to "be equal" to the calling which they—and we—have received compared to the Jews who, prior to that time, laid sole claim to being God's chosen people. Be "up to the task," Mister Gentile former craftsman of the Temple of Artemis, of being allowed into the inner sanctum of God's new Holy Temple. Even though you are not a Jew, you are now in Jesus Christ. Don't let anyone discourage you with lies that somehow you don't measure up in God's eyes.

Paul went on to tell his audience what they were supposed to do based on this call. He said in Ephesians 4:2, "Be humble and gentle. *Put up with each other in love.*"

What?

Can you imagine the response of the Gentile construction workers? "C'mon, Paul, you're stuck in jail, and we're pretty discouraged here! We're living in this cesspool of pagan idolatry, occupied by a military government from godless and cruel Rome. We're in a crisis situation and don't know what to do. We've burned our most valuable possessions to follow the message of Jesus Christ. We've got all these people, Jews and Artemis-worshippers alike, telling us we've missed the boat and angered the pagan gods, and you're saying our mission in life is to *put up* with each other?"

Yes, that's what he was saying. This new entity called "the church" was God's new plan for those who follow Him, Jew and Gentile alike, to worship in the same way, without the rituals and sacrifices of the Old Testament Law. When you consider how God's New Testament church has, since Paul's time, fragmented itself into literally hundreds of denominations, according to every interpretation of doctrine and aspect of practical worship, do you wonder how much of our power we've given up to the enemy? Today, a whole collection of books and ideas is proposing new ways to do "church." Many talk about connecting believers together in more personal ways to perform specific missions in the world around them. Implicit in these not-so-new ideas is the concept of "putting up with one another in love," celebrating and taking advantage of the power and the promises we have through our common bond in the Lord Jesus Christ. Given how often this topic is covered in the New Testament, God obviously wants His people to embrace it.

In the last three chapters of Ephesians, Paul told the New Testament Christians how we fit into God's historical plan and what we're to do in response. In Ephesians 4:7–16, he explained how each of us is given a unique and particular set of gifts or roles God wants us to fulfill. Paul gave a similar message in Romans 12:4–8 and 1 Corinthians 12:4–12. These passages give us some guidance about what to do with our lives, or what jobs we may wish to pursue. This is critical to our understanding of what it means to follow God's will. God expects us to use—and develop—the unique set of gifts, talents, interests, skills, and circumstances we possess to execute the missions He wants us to complete. We hear a lot about "spiritual gifts," but usually only as they apply when we're at church. As we continue our study, we'll see how these unique characteristics form the foundation from which God prepares us to accomplish similarly unique and specific missions tailored to us—wherever we are.

In each of his discourses on spiritual gifts, Paul never tells us how they are given out. Nor does he say how we might find out which one we possess. He leaves this to us and focuses on how we should act while we're looking for them.

This may sound less spiritual than having a "calling." The experiences of mature Christians throughout the ages indicate that God will guide each of us personally and specifically to where He wants us as His chosen instrument in a certain place. He then presents us with a choice to execute the missions He wants us to perform—or not. I've learned something else through the years: God leads us into many seemingly unrelated places and experiences we would not choose on our own. These experiences require us to make many smaller decisions that position us to make the correct major ones.

What does this mean? One of the most vivid examples from my own life took place when I went back to college, after leaving the ministry, to study electrical engineering. For several years, I tried again and again to move back to Southern California to attend a certain church. During the summer God closed the doors on my involvement in the full-time ministry, I moved out there to find a job and attend engineering school near the church.

I looked for two months and could find no job at all. Nothing. One day, I went into a particular building to fill out an application. I was told for the umpteenth time I didn't have the qualifications they were seeking. Walking away, dejected, I saw a group of newly hired engineers being warmly welcomed and escorted upstairs. I asked God, "Why am I out here looking for entry-level jobs after nine years of following you? Lord, I would already have an engineering degree had I stayed at the Air Force Academy!"

Again, silence.

Except for several phone calls I received from my mother encouraging me to move back to Texas and earn the engineering degree in my hometown, which had a chronic ten percent unemployment rate. Here was a moment of choice from God, and I knew it. In my discouragement, I felt like quitting on Him, believing it was too hard to figure out what He wanted from me. I knew quitting would not be the right thing to do. I could see this was a test, so I told God I would go home to Texas if He opened that door, and I wouldn't look back. Discouraged and unsure of what God was doing, I drove to Texas in the middle of the night. Every freeway exit I passed, I fought the urge to turn around and head back to California. But the door in Texas swung wide open: I got a job the first afternoon I started looking. This clear signal from Him provided the motivation I needed to get the engineering degree as soon as I could.

A couple of years later, still wanting to go back to California, I tried to get a summer internship with an electronics company in Los Angeles. I was not accepted to the program even though my grades and experience were better than some of those who were. Naturally, I was disappointed. Another closed door. Thinking of Paul in Acts 16:6-10, as he made plans to go to various regions and encountering one closed door after another, I was looking for someone to appear to me in a vision saying, "Come on over to California and help us!" You may find this hard to believe, but the day after the door closed again on California, I got a job offer with a similar company in Dallas. Everything looked good. It was a great company and a superb opportunity. The only thing that didn't line up for me was the location. I was getting better at recognizing open doors from God, so I went to Dallas.

Now, it wasn't clear at the time, but going there put me in contact with a group of people who planted the seeds for many things that would come to fruition in my life over the next twenty years. With their encouragement, I started thinking about earning a master's degree in business administration (MBA) from one of the top schools in the country. It also set me up for a summer job for the next three years while I completed the MBA program.

At the same time, something else was going on I wasn't made aware of until many years later. There was an undercurrent of sexual sin at the church I had wanted to attend in California. I was completely oblivious to this while I repeatedly tried to go there. I now believe, had I been there at the time, I could have gotten caught up in that sin or, because some people whom I greatly respected were involved, I might have been permanently discouraged in my faith. I'm not sure, but it seems to me now that God kept those doors closed for years to protect me from a situation I likely would not have been able to handle.

I've got to tell you, while I was moving from place to place trying to follow God's lead, squeezing through slightly open doors and smacking my head against closed ones, I began to feel like one of those shiny silver balls in a pinball machine. I asked God time and again, "Lord, where does this all lead?" It's clear to me now that those seemingly unrelated decisions set me on a different trajectory from which other, bigger decisions would come. They taught me to persevere and to trust Him day to day as these decisions came up. The move to Dallas and to business school actually lined me up for a greater opportunity in Southern California several years later, one I would not have had if I'd actually succeeded in getting one of those earlier jobs.

The ending to this story has made me appreciate God's sense of humor. After I earned my MBA, I went to work for a company in Southern California and was assigned to a project in the very same building where, years earlier, I'd applied for that job! It was as if God was saying, "Okay, Tom, you asked me several years ago why I wouldn't let you work here. Well, here you go! Welcome! Come on in!"

You may be thinking, *Hey, Tom, that's nice, but is that all?*

No, that's most definitely not all. There's another side to the story of how we fit into God's ultimate plan: our effect on those around us.

WHO IS THIS ABOUT, ANYWAY?

I'm sure you are familiar with the 1946 Frank Capra movie *It's a Wonderful Life,* mainly because it's shown on TV about a hundred times every year at Christmas. You remember George Bailey, right? He's a smart, personable, and ambitious young man with big plans for his life. He wants to be rich and famous and to live a life of adventure. Over the years, however, he has to make some difficult decisions to help those around him in their times of need. These decisions, while helpful to his friends and family, ultimately pull George away from his personal ambitions and leave him feeling stuck in his little hometown of Bedford Falls, his dreams unfulfilled.

George has struggled his entire adult life to make ends meet while, in order to stay true to his moral principles, passing up at least two big opportunities to get rich. It appears the efforts of his entire adult life have not borne any fruit let alone financial wealth. He comes to a crisis moment, a low point in his life where he's in danger of being put in jail for something that is not his fault. He considers ending it all by jumping off a bridge. His guardian angel, Clarence Oddbody, AS-2 (Angel Second Class), intervenes and jumps into the river first. George, true to form, forgets his own problems and jumps in to rescue Clarence. As they're drying off in the drawbridge operator's office, George tells Clarence he wishes he'd never been born. Clarence, being an angel, grants him his wish: George has never been born. He gets an incredible opportunity to see what Bedford Falls would be like if he'd never existed, if he'd never been there to intervene in the lives of those around him.

You've seen the movie, right? It's a startling vision. The world of Bedford Falls is plunged into greed, self-indulgence, and personal pain. Virtually all the people George knew as friends and family now have a hard and bitter edge to them. They live empty, even ruined lives, all because George wasn't there to do the little things, the good things, that helped them in their times of need.

Do you remember how the movie ends? George comes back to his real life and runs home, thankful for everything he has and everyone he sees, even though he will still likely go to jail. Suddenly, the front door of his house bursts opens, and people file in holding money in their hands. It looks like everyone George has ever helped in Bedford Falls is now walking through the door to help him. His younger brother, Harry, a Medal of Honor war hero who has just returned from meeting the President at the White House, offers a toast, "To my big brother George, the richest man in town!"

I've seen that movie about a hundred times and still get a lump in my throat when I hear Harry offer his toast. Why has *It's a Wonderful Life* been voted one of the favorite classic movies of all time? John Eldredge, in his book *Waking the Dead*, explains it well. Stories like this are so popular, he says, because they are stories God has written on our hearts. Romans 1:19–20 offers a clue about these "God stories" each of us knows deep within our soul. They are stories of redemption. We know we'd rather be like George than Mr. Potter! We appreciate Mr. Gower, the pharmacist, whose life was redeemed through a small, selfless act by George so many years before. We come to love Mrs. Bailey, his mother, and his Uncle Billy, who have been saved from financial ruin because George was there at a critical moment. We understand that Harry Bailey's accurate measure of George's true wealth comes not in dollars but in the voices and smiles of everyone singing *Auld Lang Syne* at the end of the movie. His wealth is the cumulative effect his good deeds have had on their lives.

Proverbs 22:1 says, "Choose a good reputation over great riches, for being held in high esteem is better than having silver or gold."

Do we believe that? Even though George Bailey is a make-believe character, his story is a vivid reminder of what you and I see in real life every day. Take away a certain honest and faithful person who is always there to lend a hand and the world changes in significant ways. As we'll discuss later, Satan is also at work in every workplace, church, neighborhood, and school, trying to deceive and destroy the precious souls of humanity. If we're not manning the outposts where God has placed us, the people in the world around us are in greater danger of turning toward the deceiver and to their own destruction. To paraphrase King Solomon in the book of Proverbs and in Ecclesiastes Chapters 10–12, what really matters is that you and I leave behind threads of ourselves in the lives of those with whom we've come into contact—for God's glory.

These threads extend far beyond what we can see, beyond our family and circle of close friends, to the world outside and into the distant reaches of eternity. Daniel 12:3 says, "Those who are wise will shine like the brightness of the heavens, and those who lead many to righteousness, like the stars for ever and ever." This timeless truth is something to keep in mind wherever we are. Like George Bailey, if we were removed from the picture, our absence would alter our immediate surroundings, possibly even history, in profound ways. One day, all the jobs, money, fame and influence will be gone, and only what was done for God's ultimate plan will last. "God's will for the rest of us," at least for some of us, may be to serve quietly and anonymously for years and never fully know how much we've mattered until we get to eternity. Then, as we stand and give account of our lives, we'll see the eternal effects of the little things we did, day in and day out, giving of ourselves to others and showing them the light of the Lord Jesus Christ through our fleshly bodies.

After I graduated from business school and came back to California, I worked for a company where one of my coworkers was going through a painful divorce. This individual, who was not a Christian, was under a tremendous load of stress. Trying to keep his personal life under wraps from the rest of us, he broke out with a serious skin condition. I could tell he was having major emotional problems but wasn't sure what they were. One day, while I was in his office going over some corporate accounting issues, I stopped and asked him if he was okay. Tears welled up in his eyes, and he said no. We talked for two hours that afternoon and I was able to give him some advice from the Bible and a well-known Christian author who has written several good books on marriage and relationships.

My coworker later told Kathy, "You know, Tom missed his calling. He should have been a marriage counselor." Really, I didn't miss my calling. At the time, my coworker was not in the mood for a marriage counselor. In hindsight, it's clear that God was working in his life, trying to get a message to him. At the time, he wasn't about to pay me a visit in church or in a Christian marriage counselor's office. He needed a friend who could deliver God's message to him—where he was. God sent me as His chosen instrument to deliver His message to my coworker. My calling and my mission, on that particular day, was to help my friend in his time of need.

Why there? Why me? Here's the deal: God has put His people in position all over the world as His agents, His instruments, to reach others with His message. He has placed us at work, at school, in the neighborhood, just about every place we could imagine. In some parts of the world, His agents are under severe persecution as they try to respond to the need around them. As there are so many different types of flowers, plants, and animals in God's creation, there are countless different ways He uses Christians to intervene in the circumstances of others' lives, to reach them with His message, and bring about His ultimate will. Wherever you and I happen to be is a mission field. We are given the challenge—and the choice—to involve ourselves in the work of that field.

We Christians tend to focus on "where" God wants us to be—in a certain job, in a particular city, married to a specific person—as the most important aspect of His will for our lives. We worry about being in the wrong place, potentially suffering loss of His blessings, giving up income, health, or the right spouse, because we made a wrong decision. Or we stay where we are, holding onto what we think is a sure thing, stagnated and bored, afraid to reach out and grab hold of the opportunities God brings our way.

The Bible says much about how God has promised to provide for and bless those who choose to follow Him, like David, with a pure and undivided heart. At the same time, it becomes apparent through His Word that He wants us to work for His guidance and blessing, yes, even to fight for it. It becomes apparent that His will is not just about us, but about our influence on others as His chosen special agents. Finally, it becomes clear that God wants us to think less about "where we are" and more about "what we are" while we're there. As Henry Blackaby says in his book *Experiencing God*, "God has you where you are right now for a very good reason! You are His chosen instrument for the work He's doing in that place!" This work is as sacred as any position of full-time ministry.

Kathy's best friend has cared for her mother and three husbands as they lay dying from terminal illnesses. Of all the people I know, here's a person who could ask, "Why me, God?" She has been given a special gift of service and tender compassion enabling her to be God's minister to these individuals as they spent their last days and hours on earth. Is this a "calling"? I'm sure Kathy's friend never heard a voice from God saying, "You are to be a hospice provider to sick and dying people." No, she found herself in circumstances with very sick loved ones where she was given a mission and a choice to accept it. She was given a choice to do the right thing using the gifts, temperament, and compassionate personality with which God equipped her. She chose yes, four different times. When I think of her, I think of Matthew 25:34–40:

> *Then the King will say to those on his right, "Come, you who are blessed by my Father; take your inheritance, the kingdom prepared for you since the creation of the world.*

"For I was hungry and you gave me something to eat, I was thirsty and you gave me something to drink, I was a stranger and you invited me in,

"I needed clothes and you clothed me, I was sick and you looked after me, I was in prison and you came to visit me."

Then the righteous will answer him, "Lord, when did we see you hungry and feed you, or thirsty and give you something to drink? When did we see you a stranger and invite you in, or needing clothes and clothe you? When did we see you sick or in prison and go to visit you?"

The King will reply, "I tell you the truth, whatever you did for one of the least of these brothers of mine, you did for me."

God is working in our time of history through the people of His church to reach others for His Kingdom. This is His will and His calling. God is asking us to be faithful, helping others in need as if they were the Lord Himself.

PART II:
FOUR PERSPECTIVES

Thinking about "what we should be while we're there" as we search for God's will, it might help to quickly revisit a couple of points: First, from God's point of view, each of us is where we are right now for a reason. Of course, when I say "where we are right now," I'm talking about working at such and such corporation, attending college at State U, recuperating in the hospital, or unemployed and looking for a job. It can also mean putting flowers on the grave of a loved one, getting cancer radiation treatment, receiving an award in front of hundreds of people, being stuck in traffic, or standing in the kitchen surrounded by a bunch of screaming kids.

Second, the Bible contains many illustrations of a godly, submitted, champion-level Christian life that help us understand how we should live and behave no matter where we are. The four perspectives we will study here highlight specific principles God uses through "the rest of us" to fulfill His ultimate will while, at the same time, holding us accountable for our individual decisions.

Timothy, the Apostle Paul's protégé, served as a key leader of the church of Ephesus while Paul was in his Roman jail cell. Paul wrote two letters to Timothy from there, offering a wealth of advice and encouragement to his "spiritual son." In 2 Timothy 2, Paul brought up each of these four perspectives to illustrate valuable concepts of Christian life. Beginning in verse three, he mentioned a soldier in battle, a runner in a race, a farmer in a field, and Jesus Christ's example of a sacrifice to show Timothy, and us, how to become mature and victorious Christians.

Paul referred to these four perspectives throughout his New Testament letters, as did Peter and James. They used them as references to help their readers visualize and embrace the victorious Christian life wherever they happened to be, in church or at their day jobs. The useful insights they provide us will strengthen and encourage Christians of all ages as we seek God's will and grow to spiritual maturity.

THE WARRIOR

In 2 Timothy 2:3, Paul tells Timothy to "endure hardship with us as a good soldier of Christ Jesus." The perspective of a warrior, a soldier at war, is particularly relevant to Christians today. Whether you realize it or not, we are in an ongoing battle with a treacherous and determined enemy. Satan will stop at nothing except God's power, and our own vigilance and resistance, to take us out of the fight. The "Christian-as-warrior" perspective is one of intense awareness, preparation and self-discipline, as well as strength, purpose, and victory in battle.

As we examine the Christian-as-warrior over the next few chapters, let's begin with a look at how our enemy, Satan, wages war against us. We'll follow this by exploring what the Bible says about our role in spiritual warfare. We'll learn what we can do to stand firm against the enemy's attacks and how to emerge victorious in God's plan for our lives.

DECEPTION: THE ENEMY'S
KEY TACTIC

On June 6, 1944, the Allied Expeditionary Force, an army of over 100,000 American, British, and Canadian soldiers under the command of General Dwight D. Eisenhower, invaded the continent of Europe. Called Operation OVERLORD by the military planners, this was the most significant offensive military campaign by the Allies against Nazi Germany in World War II, and is known today simply as D-Day. It is not well known that the Allied forces conducted another major military operation against Germany at the same time. This second operation, called FORTITUDE, commanded by Lieutenant General George Patton, was one of the largest military deceptions in history. The intent of this operation was to make the German high command think that OVERLORD, the main Allied invasion of the Normandy beaches, was simply a diversion.

Operation FORTITUDE was an elaborate deception scheme built around fake radio transmissions, dummy vehicles, false documents, and carefully orchestrated "sightings" by double agents. FORTITUDE reinforced the German High Command's belief that the main invasion would come at the Pas de Calais, the point in France closest to England, where the Eurotunnel entrance exists today. Adolf Hitler and his military staff were so convinced FORTITUDE was the main Allied attack, they withheld the *Wehrmacht* Fifteenth Army, a force of over 100,000 well-trained fighting troops, in the Pas de Calais while the Allied forces came ashore at Normandy and fought their way inland. By the time the Germans realized their mistake, the Allies had established a beachhead on the European mainland and were moving significant reinforcements ashore. It was too late.

This story is one of many from history showing why deception is an effective weapon in the military commander's arsenal. The ancient Chinese philosopher Sun Tzu, one of history's most influential military strategists, wrote in *The Art of War* that the "acme of skill" in warfare is to defeat an enemy without a fight. If a combat commander can trick his opponent into deploying his forces in the wrong place, or worse, if he can infiltrate his adversary's forces and weaken them without waging an actual fight, he can overcome the opponent with fewer forces of his own.

Does this sound familiar? To realize the full extent of Jesus Christ's victory over Satan on the cross, let's look at Colossians 2:13-15:

When you were dead in your sins and in the uncircumcision of your sinful nature, God made you alive with Christ.

He forgave us all our sins, having canceled the written code, with its regulations, that was against us and that stood opposed to us; he took it away, nailing it to the cross.

And having disarmed the powers and authorities, he made a public spectacle of them, triumphing over them by the cross.

God completely defeated Satan at the cross and publicly disarmed the enemy forces in the spiritual world. As a result, Satan and his demons have only one effective weapon to use against Christians today: deception. Jesus Christ, Paul, Peter, and James warned us to not be deceived. In 2 Corinthians 2:11, Paul said of Satan, "We are wise to his schemes." He mentioned Satan's "snare" three times in his two letters to Timothy and warned the Corinthian church that Satan himself is transformed into an angel of light—an elaborate and effective deception if there ever was one.

Jesus spoke of Satan in John 8:44:

There is no truth in him. When he lies, he speaks his native language, for he is a liar and the father of lies.

In Genesis 3, Satan seduced Eve with a lie, a deception about what God had said concerning the forbidden fruit. Deception started the chain of events that brought about the fallen, sinful world you and I live in today. According to the Bible, a person redeemed in Jesus Christ is secure in his or her salvation. The children of God in Jesus Christ are sealed until the day of redemption (2 Corinthians 1:22, Ephesians 1:13 and 4:30) through His victory on the cross. 1 Peter 1:5 (KJV) tells us we are "kept by the power of God through faith unto salvation ready to be revealed in the last time." This doesn't mean Satan cannot trick us into taking ourselves out of the fight, squandering our usefulness to God's ultimate plan. Satan has no power to destroy us—unless we willingly give it to him. Paul makes reference to the "destruction of the flesh" in 1 Corinthians 5:5, which is the only way Satan is able to "destroy" a Christian. Here is the key: Satan is constantly trying to get us into a position where we'll relinquish control of our hearts to him through our own fleshly desires. Doing so allows him to deceive us and lure us into compromising situations that reduce or eliminate our effectiveness for God.

Proverbs 19:3 in the New Living Translation (NLT) says, "People ruin their lives by their own foolishness and then are angry at the Lord." Worse, Satan can deceive Christians into committing acts of treason, doing things that help him lead those around us away from the truth to their own destruction.

YES, WE ARE AT WAR

How do we protect ourselves against Satan's schemes of deception? Karl von Clausewitz, the famous nineteenth-century Prussian military strategist, called war the ultimate "contest of wills." Even though Satan was defeated on the cross, God in His sovereign will has allowed him to remain on the loose until a specific point in the future (Revelation 20:1). As a consequence, you and I must fight his deceptions as an ongoing part of our Christian experience. You may have read some of the many useful books on spiritual warfare that are available today. Most of them discuss the "whole armor of God" from Ephesians 6:11 and "weapons of our warfare" in 2 Corinthians 10:4. At the same time, Jesus Christ and Paul referred to several other aspects of warfare that aren't so readily apparent.

Over the course of my career, I've trained with a number of military combat units, law enforcement officials, and counterterrorism experts. Every training session shared a common theme: "Train like you fight." The training experts advise military organizations and law enforcement agencies to train their "operators" under pressure. Standing on a firing range, well rested, shoulders squared, one eye shut, and taking your time to shoot at a round, stationary target doesn't prepare you for the indescribably intense pressure of having to defend yourself and those around you against an armed opponent who is trying to kill you.

Elite military and law enforcement operators train as much as they can under intense and realistic pressure because they know they won't have time to figure it out in an actual confrontation. They need to know instinctively how to perform in the decisive moment of contact with the enemy. There's only one chance to get it right. The training experts also hammer home this point: the most significant weapon you have is your *mind*. Being mentally prepared to defend yourself at the critical moment is the most important part of going up against a determined, armed enemy.

Why do I bring this up? C. S. Lewis, the great Christian philosopher and writer, said we are living in enemy-occupied territory. According to Ephesians 2:2, Satan is the "prince of the power of the air," and Paul, in 2 Corinthians 4:4, calls him "the god of this world." Satan is a real enemy who is actively and ruthlessly working against everything we hold dear. Whether we admit it or not, we are in a real war. Stu Weber, in his book *Spirit Warriors*, calls it "battlefield earth." In military terms, not only are we in enemy territory, we are "in contact." We are engaged in actual, close-quarters combat with our enemy. As 1 Peter 5:8 warns us, Satan is like a roaring lion, prowling around and looking for someone to swallow whole. He is fully intent on striking us at our center of gravity, the core of our spiritual strength, to neutralize our effectiveness as instruments of God's ultimate plan.

What is the core of our spiritual strength? It is the level of our commitment to the Lord Jesus Christ. It is our desire, our will, to follow Him through enemy-occupied territory to storm Satan's fortress and emerge victorious in the battle against him. Without this commitment, we leave ourselves open to the enemy's deceptions and cannot be effective warriors for Christ. As we've seen before, God is going to prevail in this ultimate battle of the ages but will hold us accountable for our individual decisions. The question is whether we will join the fight and be part of His winning army.

I know Christians who would rather deny that Satan actually exists or hope he'll leave them alone. To quote a well-known former senator who lectured an army general a few years ago during the hearings on the Iraq war, "Hope is not a strategy." The general's response was, "Yes, but neither is despair." Both comments apply to you and me in this real war in which we find ourselves. We can't hope Satan will go away and leave us alone. He won't. But we shouldn't despair and think we're defenseless against his attacks and schemes of deception. We're not.

Satan tries to attack Christians individually when and where we are weakest. He plays on our desires, fears, guilt, insecurities, and especially our pride. A critical point needs to be made here: if we're out on our own, living our lives away from the protection and accountability of a fellowship of believers, we're an easy, slow-moving target for him to pick off. There's strength in numbers. God instituted fellowship and accountability in His *ekklesia,* or "assembly," the Greek word for "church," to provide us that collective strength.

Because he knows what spiritual power can be unleashed when Christians assemble together, Satan tries to take down entire churches and bodies of believers. During my four years at the Bible college, I traveled with the school's choral singing group to over four hundred churches. In far too many of them, I witnessed internal power struggles that ended in church splits or in the pastor being forced to resign in disgrace while the people of the congregation, wounded and disillusioned, scattered in all directions.

Why does this happen? I believe these churches forgot, or never realized, that they are outposts in enemy territory. They were like the young platoon leader in E.D. Swinton's military classic, *The Defense of Duffer's Drift.* This young infantry officer set up camp in enemy territory but failed to prepare his outpost for the inevitable enemy attack. He and his men were ambushed and defeated. Strength in numbers has no meaning if the military unit isn't ready to do battle. Like a camp full of soldiers who've fallen asleep without posting guards, these churches became focused on their own internal politics and left their perimeter undefended against Satan's subtle yet brutal assault. They were attacked and defeated, taken out of the fight.

Effective military commanders who are operating in enemy territory constantly assess the battlefield situation, trying to understand what is happening around them. They send out reconnaissance patrols to find the enemy's location and assess the strength of his forces. They use the surrounding terrain to their advantage. These commanders remain acutely sensitive to enemy deceptions. If their own attacks against the enemy are going too easily, or if the enemy is leaving them alone, their sixth sense kicks in and the hair on the back of their neck stands up. They look closely to see if the enemy is purposely drawing them in with a deception in order to hammer them from another direction.

To repeat what Paul said in 2 Corinthians 2:11, "We are wise to [Satan's] schemes." We know the enemy's objective to deceive us and take us out of the fight. We know his tactics, which are all based on lies, his native language. Our effective response in battling the devil is to strengthen our spiritual instincts so we can perform as victorious Christians in the critical moments of decision, when we're in contact with the enemy. When we're asking God for directions, we must be aware that Satan and his demons will be right there, lying to us and trying to steer us off course away from Him. They want to neutralize our effectiveness and cheat us out of our reward. We need to post guard around our own hearts and on the perimeter of our churches.

Most importantly, to effectively resist the devil's schemes, we must recognize the basic principles of warfare the Bible uses to help us fight and prevail against our enemy.

PRINCIPLES OF WARFARE

Not too long ago, I completed a course of study for senior military officers at the Naval War College. This course included a detailed review of the overall principles of warfare and emphasized how important planning is to the military commander conducting a successful battle campaign. The first thing I learned was the three levels of warfare: the *strategic*, the *operational* and the *tactical*. A senior commander has to consider all three levels when planning to go to war against an enemy. Let's take a look at something Jesus Christ said in Luke 14:31–32:

> *Suppose a king is about to go to war against another king. Will he not first sit down and consider whether he is able with ten thousand men to oppose the one coming against him with twenty thousand?*

> *If he is not able, he will send a delegation while the other is still a long way off and will ask for terms of peace.*

The king in Jesus' story is about to go to war against a better armed enemy. If he's going to win, he's got to take a serious look at a few things. First, the king has to review his *strategy*: does it make sense to go to war or to use diplomacy instead? Both are effective instruments of national policy and rational alternatives for the king to consider. If the king decides to go to war, he must evaluate certain things as part of his strategy. What will bring victory? What are the enemy's key weaknesses? Do I have the resources to fight him? Can I form alliances with other kings to help me go to war against him?

Next, he and his military commanders consider a number of *operational* questions based on the strategy. What will our military campaign look like? How will we deploy our troops? Can we rely on terrain, deception, surprise, and speed to overcome our enemy's numerical advantage? Can we force the enemy to split his forces into smaller units that cannot support each other? What about resupplying our troops over long distances?

When the king and his military leaders have answered these questions, the commanders come up with the *tactical* battle plan for this operational campaign. They give instructions to their soldiers to execute the battle plan: cross this river at this location, on this night, and get to the objective before dawn. Use deception to entice the enemy to mass his forces over here by this terrain feature. Attack his exposed flanks from the other direction and reinforce with the reserve force upon our signal. Press the attack until you break through his lines and capture his headquarters.

Each of the Old Testament "historical books," from Joshua through 2 Chronicles, describes battle plans the armies of Israel used against their enemies. For example, in 2 Samuel 5:23–24 and 1 Chronicles 14:14–15, God gave King David a *tactical* battle plan that included deception and a flanking attack in front of a grove of balsam trees. The *operational* level of the battle was God's plan to use David to eliminate all of Israel's enemies so his son, Solomon, could rule in peace and build God's Temple in Jerusalem (1 Chronicles 22:6–10). The *strategic* level was God's covenant promises to Abraham, Jacob, Joseph, Moses, and David to make Israel a great, chosen nation on the earth by which all nations would be blessed (Genesis 22:18 and 26:4, Deuteronomy 26:19, 1 Chronicles 16:31), and through which the Redeemer would come (Genesis 49:10).

We can see God's strategic and operational plans for battling Satan in our time. In Ephesians 3:1–12, Paul tells us God waited to reveal His strategy for the New Testament church until after the death, burial, and resurrection of His Son, Jesus Christ. Until then, God's strategy was classified "Top Secret" in heaven and on earth. Paul called it a "mystery," and in Colossians 1:26, said it was hidden from ages and generations. He described this secret strategy as God's call to Jews and Gentiles to join Him as fellow-citizens together in the assembly of believers who make up the household of God (Ephesians 2:19). To get a sense of how big a deal this was to the Jews, take a look at Luke 4:16–30, where Jesus opened his ministry in His hometown of Nazareth. In his debut sermon to the home crowd, he gave a broad hint that the Gentiles might be included in God's ultimate plan. That sermon ended with His long-time friends and neighbors trying to toss him over a cliff!

In Ephesians 1:9–11, Paul says Jesus Christ revealed this "Top Secret" strategy, in the fullness of time, by announcing it to the rulers and authorities in the heavenly realms. These are the same demonic rulers and authorities He operationally disarmed when, as we saw in Colossians 2:15, He made a public spectacle of His triumph over them on the cross. Another key operational aspect of the Lord's ultimate plan is revealed in 1 John 3:8:

> *He who does what is sinful is of the devil, because the devil has been sinning from the beginning. The reason the Son of God appeared was to destroy the devil's work.*

Ephesians 3:1–12 and Colossians 1:26–27 tell us God is executing His ultimate plan in our time of world history through His church. For reasons known only to Him, God expects you and me to fight against the same rulers and authorities, the powers of darkness and spiritual forces of evil in heavenly places. This is clearly stated in Ephesians 6:12. What does it mean to struggle against these enemy forces? Obviously we struggle with them over the sin that can so easily ensnare us, but I also believe we fight with them over the missions God gives to us. In 1 Thessalonians 2:18, Paul tells his readers Satan hindered his plans to return to visit them. Yes, God expects us to struggle against these disarmed rulers and authorities.

Many Christians use verses like Proverbs 21:30–31 to justify not making plans or preparations for their life in the Lord:

> *There is no wisdom, no insight, no plan that can succeed against the Lord.*

The horse is made ready for the day of battle, but victory rests with the Lord.

They say, "God's in control. He'll do the job the way He wants, so any plans or preparations I make will be wasted." Well, that may sound nice and pious, but it's not true. It is Satan's oldest deception: using God's Word against us. I once attended a seminar on goal setting and time management where I heard the speaker say, "Most people spend more time planning their next vacation than they do the rest of their lives." One maxim we hear over and over again in the military is, "Fail to plan, plan to fail." Even though God closed a lot of doors on Paul in Acts Chapter 16, He didn't stop him from planning or minimize the importance of doing so.

If we as Christ's followers ignore the need to plan, and instead wait for what we think is some sign from Him, we can easily be led astray through a deception of Satan. We might succumb to his deception of fear and follow the path of least resistance, giving up the opportunity to step out in bold faith. At the other extreme, as mentioned in James 4:13–17, we might make boastful plans and leave God out of the approval chain, only to be deceived into pursuing a course of action that strokes our own pride or leads us to follow a false god. We may actually make plans but become discouraged to quit by more of Satan's lies. A strong, mature, warrior-minded Christian follows the example of the Lord Jesus Christ, who often retreated by himself to commune with His Father, to lay his or her plans before Him. Resisting the forces of darkness in God's power, he or she carries them out in His strength.

THE WEAPONS OF OUR WARFARE

If you've done a Bible study on spiritual warfare, you are likely familiar with Ephesians 6:13–17. Here, Paul refers to a similar passage in Isaiah 59:17 and tells us to put on the belt of truth, the breastplate (or body armor) of righteousness, the shoes of the preparation of the gospel of peace, the shield of faith, the helmet of salvation and the sword of the Spirit, which is the Word of God.

As someone who has served in a combat zone, I can vouch for the importance of strong defensive armor and effective offensive weaponry. In Paul's analogy, the belt of truth holds everything together. In a world where many people believe there is no absolute truth, the mature Christian stands out as someone who can hold on to the absolute truth of Jesus Christ and resist the destructive lies of Satan. As Jesus said in John 14:6, "I am the way, the truth, and the life. No one comes to the Father but by me."

The breastplate of righteousness protects our bodies from incoming attacks. It is the righteousness of God transferred to us through Jesus Christ, the justification we have through our salvation in Him. Romans 5:18 says, "Consequently, just as the result of one trespass [Adam's sin] was condemnation for all men, so also the result of one act of righteousness [Christ's victory on the cross] was justification that brings life for all men." This justification protects the core of our being in Christ. We are protected from the judgment God will pronounce on those who have rejected Him, those whose names are not written in the book of life (John 5:24, Revelation 20:15). With the breastplate of God's righteousness, we can withstand Satan's accusations and lies when they penetrate our outer defenses.

The shoes, which usually get glossed over in most studies about the armor of God, are the foundation of our preparation in the gospel of Jesus Christ.

They are important enough to discuss separately in the next chapter. The shield of faith defends us from the "fiery arrows" of the enemy. If you've seen the movies *Braveheart* or *Gladiator*, you understand how terrifying it could be for a soldier, standing on a field of battle and trying to protect himself against incoming, flaming arrows. I believe Satan's flaming arrows are those lies he uses to terrify or discourage us, trying to get us to break ranks in retreat and render ourselves of no value in the battle. Romans 5:1 says, "Therefore, since we have been justified through faith, we have peace with God through our Lord Jesus Christ." Our faith is the means through which we've been justified in Jesus Christ, and Satan can only try to deceive us into thinking otherwise. 1 Corinthians 16:13 says, "Be on your guard; stand firm in the faith; be men of courage; be strong."

The next piece of equipment is the helmet of salvation, again taken from Isaiah 59:17 and mentioned in 1 Thessalonians 5:8. Many spiritual warfare books talk about how the helmet obviously protects the head. If it gets injured, we're out of the fight. Interestingly, Paul tells us in 1 Thessalonians 5:8 to wear "the hope of salvation" as our helmet. What does this mean? John MacArthur, in his comprehensive book called *The Believer's Armor,* explains how we Christians will one day be delivered from the presence of sin. This hope of complete salvation in Jesus Christ keeps us focused on our mission during our battles against Satan. It enables us to remain on our guard and stand firm in the faith, sober and vigilant.

Next, Paul mentions the sword of the Spirit, which is the Word of God. This point can't be emphasized strongly enough: a soldier must know how to use his weapon. Without this knowledge, he is worse than useless. He's dangerous to himself and his fellow soldiers. I know firsthand stories of soldiers who were killed in battle because they thought they were cooks or mechanics first and warriors second. The Marine Corps drums into every new recruit, "Every Marine a rifleman." They learn *My Rifle: The Creed of a U.S. Marine,* written in World War II by Major General William H. Rupertus:

This is my rifle. There are many like it, but this one is mine. My rifle is my best friend. It is my life. I must master it as I master my life.

My rifle, without me, is useless. Without my rifle, I am useless. I must fire my rifle true. I must shoot straighter than my enemy who is trying to kill me. I must shoot him before he shoots me.

I will ...

Because a warrior may not know when or where the enemy will attack, his weapon must be clean, oiled, loaded with ammunition, and ready for use. The warrior must know how to use it and must develop this proficiency through regular practice. In ancient times, the sword was an offensive and defensive weapon. Hebrews 4:12 says the Word of God is alive and full of energy, and sharper than any two-edged sword (the most powerful individual weapon of war available in his day). It is able to cut all the way to the bone and is a discerner of the thoughts and intents of the heart.

Our success in the spiritual battles being waged around us depends on our ability to use the Word of God as an offensive and defensive weapon. When Satan is using his lies and schemes to take us out of the fight, we Christian warriors need to be proficient with our weapon, cutting to the core of the enemy's attacks and discerning the thoughts and intents of the heart. These would not only be the thoughts and intents of people around us but also, and more importantly, of our own hearts. May we work as seriously to master the Word of God as the Marine does his rifle.

Another dimension of our weapons of war is not covered in many other books on this subject. Let's look at 2 Corinthians 10:3–6, a familiar passage in which Paul uses specific military terms to make a point to a group of disobedient church members:

For though we walk in the flesh, we do not war after the flesh: (For the weapons of our warfare are not carnal, but mighty through God to the pulling down of strong holds;)

Casting down imaginations, and every high thing that exalteth itself against the knowledge of God, and bringing into captivity every thought to the obedience of Christ;

And having in a readiness to revenge all disobedience, when your obedience is fulfilled.

This passage is a useful guide to understand how we wage spiritual warfare against the enemy. The Greek words in this passage are actual military terms used to describe ancient warfare. As Stu Weber describes thoroughly in *Spirit Warriors*, an ancient kingdom or city would build a stronghold, or fortress, from which it could withstand an enemy's attack and where the people of the kingdom could retreat for protection. The fortress would have a set of bulwarks positioned around the walls, elevated towers from where soldiers could watch the horizon for the enemy's approach.

In this passage, Paul essentially describes a tactical battle plan to attack and destroy a major fortified enemy position. The fortress is *pulled down* (taken down and demolished), the towers are *cast down* (thrown down from above), the people inside are *brought into captivity*, and *revenge* is taken upon the disobedient ones (the ringleaders of the opposing kingdom). According to Paul's description, the attacking forces are on the move, completely offensive in their execution, hitting the enemy's strongholds with extreme, violent force.

How many times have you heard Christian spiritual warfare described like that?

Does this mean we should go out looking for a fight with the devil or with those groups who oppose Christians? No, not in our own power. In the grand scheme of God's ultimate plan, such a tactical effort would likely be outside his strategic and operational plans. It would be like mounting a pinprick suicide charge against a well-fortified enemy. It would be wasted, or worse, counterproductive.

We must keep in mind the importance of planning to make sure our tactical efforts fit into God's strategic and operational campaigns. We cannot overemphasize the importance of guarding against deception. If Satan can get us to expend ourselves in a non-productive attack, he's taken us out of the fight and rendered us useless to the broader war effort. Paul reminds us in 2 Corinthians 10:4 that the weapons of our warfare (literally our "campaign" or "expedition") are spiritual and not of the flesh. This is obviously very important, but what does it mean? How has God actually equipped us in the Spirit to, as Stu Weber says, "close with and fight the enemy"?

The word used here for "weapons" is the Greek *hopla*, from which comes the military word "hoplite." In the ancient Greek and Roman armies, the hoplites were frontline infantry shock troops the commander used to breach the enemy's strongest formations. The hoplites were from the middle class, men of financial means, who bought their weapons and armor with their own money. I find this quite interesting. Do you think there's a connection here with maintaining our own spiritual weaponry and armor in order to voluntarily join the frontline shock troops of God's army, to be one whom our Commander relies on to break through the enemy's strongest formations?

The Lord covers the entire spectrum of battlefield preparations from which we are able, through Him, to conduct successful combat operations against the enemy. Nahum 1:7 in the New American Standard Bible (NASB) tells us "the Lord is good, a stronghold in the day of trouble, and He knows those who take refuge in Him." Psalm 61 says the Lord is our high tower and a "rock higher than I," meaning He is like a place of refuge in a high cliff for a bird, safe from its predators. Chuck Holton wrote a book called *Bulletproof* that was a great source of encouragement to me when I deployed to Iraq with the

U.S. Marine Corps in 2006. Enduring rocket attacks in Baghdad and flying in military helicopters over enemy-held territory in the middle of the night, with the real and immediate possibility of getting shot at by small arms fire or shoulder-fired surface-to-air missiles, I often thought about the point he made in this book:

Nothing can harm a Christian without God's direct permission.

In God's ultimate, sovereign will, nothing takes Him by surprise. At the same time, he has subjected His children to the physical limitations, evils, and dangers of this world. He has also promised He'll never leave us or forsake us (Hebrews 13:5). We don't have to be afraid, and we don't have to lash out in our own power against the enemy. God is giving us the battle plans through our close walk with Him. David, the warrior king, the man after God's own heart, wrote in Psalm 27:1–3:

The Lord is my light and my salvation—whom shall I fear? The Lord is the stronghold of my life   of whom shall I be afraid?

When evil men advance against me to devour my flesh, when my enemies and my foes attack me, they will stumble and fall.

Though an army besiege me, my heart will not fear; though war break out against me, even then will I be confident.

He wrote this in Psalm 18:2 (KJV):

The Lord is my rock, and my fortress, and my deliverer; my God, my strength, in whom I will trust; my buckler [shield], and the horn of my salvation, and my high tower.

Like Paul, David used specific military terms to describe God's complete and comprehensive array of protection for His followers. God, our rock and fortress, is where we go for safety and sustenance when we feel overwhelmed by the enemy. God Himself is our deliverer, our shield, and the horn (strength) of our salvation when we're on the attack. He is our high tower, from which we can see the entire battlefield and discover the enemy's route of advance before he can launch his attack against us.

As Chuck Holton points out, we can take comfort in knowing that 366 Bible verses tell God's children not to be afraid. God decides when and how we'll leave this life, and how we'll suffer for Him. We do battle in the power of the Lord, not in our own strength, as the frontline soldiers in His ultimate, expeditionary battle campaign against Satan.

As for our offensive spiritual firepower, it helps to consider what military and law enforcement agencies call "escalation of force." In the military context, this doctrine provides the commander a range of options from "presence" to "total war," with the objective of using appropriate force to influence or change the adversary's intentions in our favor. The United States Navy, for example, has patrolled the world's oceans for many years practicing a doctrine called "forward presence." The appearance of a group of warships on the horizon has deterred many potential conflicts and acts of aggression. If an adversary decides to counter the presence of the warships and escalate the conflict, the commander may conduct aggressive maneuvers against the adversary's ships to indicate the seriousness of his position. From there, the warship may fire warning shots and, lastly, resort to lethal force. Ground forces have recently adopted similar escalation of force measures in the highly politicized and televised counterinsurgency environments of Iraq and Afghanistan. These tactics more closely resemble law enforcement practices than historical military doctrine.

Effective escalation of force is carried out only through a deliberate thought process and well-defined "rules of engagement." 1 Peter 5:8–9 says,

Be self-controlled and alert. Your enemy the devil prowls around like a roaring lion looking for someone to devour.

Resist him, standing firm in the faith, because you know that your brothers throughout the world are undergoing the same kind of sufferings.

Doesn't this sound like Paul's warning in 1 Corinthians 16:3? Being self-controlled and alert keeps us aligned with God's battle plans and aware of Satan's deceptive schemes. Peter makes it clear this is not about hiding inside the fortress, hoping the enemy will go away. But it's also not about lashing out and expending ourselves against the forces of darkness in a blind, emotional, and reactive state of mind apart from God's strategic and operational battle plans. Rather, it is a series of planned and controlled actions designed to bring about a desired end state with an appropriate and effective amount of force. As Stu Weber says in *Spirit Warriors*, the Lord is looking for warriors, not brawlers.

OUR RULES OF ENGAGEMENT: STAND AND SHINE

Rules of engagement are defined across the spectrum of warfare. These rules serve to keep the fighting units aligned to the broader goals of the campaign. Every soldier is expected to know them: when to engage the enemy, when to hold fire, what to do with prisoners and how to provide humanitarian assistance to non-combatants.

When I served in the army before I went to Bible college, I was an air cavalry scout in an armored cavalry regiment. The regiment was a highly mobile, stand-alone combat unit of over 3,500 soldiers. It was the forward reconnaissance element for a much larger combat force of three infantry and armored divisions. Our rules of engagement instructed us to conduct helicopter reconnaissance patrols into enemy territory. Our objective was to find the enemy's forces and make contact, deny his ability to maneuver, and then call in the heavier armor and infantry units to decisively engage him. We shortened this to, "Find him, fix him, and finish him."

Our small group of scout aviators was the most forward deployed friendly unit, essentially the "tip of the tip of the spear." I didn't fully appreciate this until much later, but we were using tactics dating back to ancient times. For centuries, battlefield commanders used horse cavalry as highly mobile scouts to patrol ahead of friendly units to find the enemy and report back on his dispositions. Our helicopters replaced the horses, giving us even greater range, mobility, and speed. The cavalry also served as shock troops, often showing up at an unexpected place where the enemy was unprepared to respond. This mobile attack force gave the friendly commander an opportunity to create and exploit the enemy's momentary chaos, deny his ability to maneuver, attack *en masse* with heavier forces at his weakest points, and seize the victory.

Not long ago, I was reading the Bible and came across a familiar and simple instruction in Ephesians 4:27 (KJV). Upon closer inspection, it revealed a deeper meaning in the context of our spiritual rules of engagement:

Neither give place to the devil.

The words "give place" come from a Greek phrase also translated "make room" or "give a foothold." More specifically, the Greek word for "place" is *topos,* from which we get the words "topography" or "topological." *Topos* speaks of maps and terrain. This takes on major significance in the Christian-as-warrior perspective. Another way to translate this verse is: "Don't give ground to the devil."

Giving and taking ground are terms often used to describe military battles. Since the dawn of history, military commanders have studied maps of their battlefield to find ways to use the surrounding terrain to their advantage. Sun Tzu, the ancient Chinese military strategist, warned military leaders to pay close attention to the principles of terrain, saying, "The general who has attained a responsible post must be careful to study them." As they move toward the enemy, wise military commanders follow a related rule of engagement: "Take the high ground." This saying, also from Sun Tzu, advises the commander to seize and occupy the highest points on the battlefield. From there, the commander can see the enemy's movements and more effectively direct the course of the battle.

A scene in the movie *Patton* shows a British general asking the American commander if he shouldn't fall back and regroup rather than immediately attack. General Patton responds, "Not me, Freddie, I don't believe in paying for the same real estate twice." Giving ground to the enemy surrenders the advantage to him in choosing the time and place of attack and the amount of force he'll have to use. We want to keep those advantages for ourselves. The most effective way to do that is to take and hold the high ground.

If we Christians are to control the tempo of our battle in the spiritual realms, we must push forward and occupy the terrain around us to find and fix the enemy. This means getting outside the safe confines of our fortress and patrolling the countryside to locate the enemy's positions and to deny him the ability to maneuver against us. Fundamentally, we must discern the enemy's motives and plans as early and as far away from the home base as possible. As Paul says in 2 Corinthians 2:11, we need to be wise to Satan's schemes and not let him outsmart us.

We can prepare the battleground in prayer and call in the spiritual heavy armor for the upcoming battle. As Daniel 10:10–13 suggests, our prayers energize the angelic forces doing battle in the heavenly realms on our behalf, and work in concert with the power of the Holy Spirit to execute our part of God's New Testament battle campaign according to His rules of engagement. We want to force Satan to react to us. When God gives us our mission orders, we'll be able to execute them effectively without being tricked, outsmarted, or hindered by the enemy.

Does this sound to you at all like the twenty-first century church?

Unfortunately, many churches and individual Christians have adopted a passive, defensive, and comfort-oriented mindset in their walk with the Lord. They spend as much time as they can in the safety of the church building, which by no accident is called the "sanctuary," hoping nothing bad will happen to them while the enemy lays waste to the terrain outside. When they do go outside they are invisible, hiding their light under a basket. Or worse, they are aiding and abetting the enemy. 2 Kings 18:27 and Isaiah 36:12 contain disturbing and graphic depictions of what happens when people hunker down inside the fortress for too long and allow the enemy to control the terrain outside.

James 4:7 says, "Resist the devil and he will flee from you." The Greek word for "flee" means "run away fast." The word translated here as "resist" is also used in the spiritual warfare verses of 1 Peter 5:9 and Ephesians 6:13. It means to stand our ground, to actively and firmly oppose the powers of darkness. It's not a passive term. Paul used the word "stand" four times when he talks about the armor of God in Ephesians 6:11–14. Obviously, he wanted to make sure we didn't miss the point.

Modern armies fight with tanks, helicopters, and precision-guided munitions dropped from unmanned air vehicles instead of with swords, shields, and arrows. Because of this, many contemporary Bible commentaries and books on spiritual warfare overlook the important, ancient military principle of standing one's ground. Greek and Roman armies fought in formations of troops standing close to one another and executing well-coordinated movements against the enemy. The most important thing a soldier could do was maintain his place in the formation, in essence, to stand. If he fell down, he was finished. He would now be a danger to his fellow soldiers because of the empty place he left in their formation, a hole through which the enemy could penetrate. His fellow soldiers would stumble over his bloody body as they tried to maneuver against the enemy.

This is one reason why Paul listed shoes in Ephesians 6:15 as a critical part of the full armor of God: "And with your feet fitted with the readiness that comes from the gospel of peace." In this verse, the word "readiness" can be translated as "preparation of a firm foundation." The firm foundation allows us to stand in the battle and not fall down. Paul implies that we prepare our foundation by learning and understanding the gospel, or good news, of Jesus Christ's victory on the cross. As the old, classic hymn aptly says:

> How firm a foundation, ye saints of the Lord, is laid for your faith in His excellent Word.

The ancient soldier's role, standing in formation and wearing his battle armor, was to execute the mission as directed by the commander. His responsibility was to actively resist the enemy. The commander was responsible for positioning and maneuvering the overall formation to gain maximum advantage against the enemy. Thucydides, the ancient Greek historian, tells how the Spartans struck terror in the enemy's hearts by marching onto the battlefield. Their precise, interlocked formations and well-executed tactics literally shook the ground. The hoplites, the shock troops at the front, would plow into the enemy with unbelievable, almost unstoppable force.

You may wonder what we Christians are supposed to do when we make contact with the enemy. Besides standing our ground against the enemy, actively resisting in the faith (Ephesians 6:13, James 4:7, and 1 Peter 5:9), Paul brings up the spiritual concept of "presence." He refers to this in several of his New Testament letters as he advises us how to conduct our tactical battles with Satan. In Philippians 2:15 (KJV), he encourages us to be "blameless and harmless, the sons of God, without rebuke, in the midst of a crooked and perverse nation, among whom ye shine as lights in the world." In Romans 13:12, he tells us to "cast off the works of darkness, and let us put on the armor of light."

What is this "light?" It is the glory and power of God, represented within our bodies in the face of Jesus Christ. Paul wonderfully describes it in 2 Corinthians 4:6–7:

> For God, who said, "Let light shine out of darkness," made his light shine in our hearts to give us the light of the knowledge of the glory of God in the face of Christ.

> But we have this treasure in jars of clay [our earthly bodies] to show that this all-surpassing power is from God and not from us.

This is about being an instrument, an agent of moral clarity, and a conduit of God's power. It's about standing in His formation of other believers and angelic powers and shining the light of His glory in the workplace and community where He has placed us. It is about allowing God to use us as His most forward deployed sentinels of presence in enemy-held territory. In Ephesians 5:8–11, Paul told the Gentile Christian trade workers:

For you were once darkness, but now you are light in the Lord. Live as children of light (for the fruit of the light consists in all goodness, righteousness and truth) and find out what pleases the Lord.

Have nothing to do with the fruitless deeds of darkness, but rather expose them.

This offensive weapon of "presence" in the Christian warrior's spiritual arsenal, the light of Jesus Christ, is exercised in the power of the Holy Spirit. It is God's designated weapon to expose, or in our rules of engagement parlance, "fix" the works of darkness. Paul continues his explanation of "light" in Ephesians 5:13–17:

Everything exposed by the light becomes visible, for it is light that makes everything visible.

Be very careful, then, how you live—not as unwise but as wise, making the most of every opportunity, because the days are evil.

Therefore do not be foolish, but understand what the Lord's will is.

Paul said in Ephesians 5:13 that light makes everything visible. If you're in a dark room and light a candle, everyone in the room can see the light. Darkness can't hide it. Louis Brandeis, a famous Supreme Court Justice in the early twentieth century, once said, "Sunshine is the best disinfectant." He meant that shining the light of law enforcement or media attention on dark, corrupt practices is the best way to expose and clean them up. Think about how many corrupt backroom deals have been made in corporations and government to give unfair advantage or money to certain groups. In the early 1990s, former New York City police chief William Bratton engineered a major turnaround in crime on the streets of that big city through his "broken window" theory of law enforcement. Adopted from a March, 1982 article in *The Atlantic* magazine, his efforts focused on cleaning up the little things: petty theft, vandalism, and vagrancy. As a result, the bigger crimes, such as murder, robbery, and rape, declined precipitously. Shining light into dark places helped clean up the city and dramatically reduce the crime rate.

Think about this: how many times has someone in your workplace or neighborhood assumed, without any prior knowledge about your faith, that you are a Christian? People have come up to ask me if I'm a believer, without any prompting on my part, enough times for me to become sensitive to it. I've also become sensitive to situations where God brings together two or three Christians into a particular workplace or into the life of a specific individual. It's as if He's ganging up on that place, or that person, and is a sure sign that He's getting ready to do a work with eternal consequences. Each of the Christians He's brought into that place has an opportunity, and a choice, to participate in the mission or to ignore it.

In Ephesians 5:15–16, Paul warns us to be careful how we live, and to make the most of the opportunities placed before us to participate in the missions God gives us. The Greek word for "make the most" literally means to "buy back" our time, to make it count. God has stationed people like you and me in different places to be the "presence of light," His ambassadors, to help the people in those places understand that He not only loves them so much He gave His Son to die for them, but is watching what they're doing, and will hold them to account. In my business career, I've seen what happens when God removes His people from a workplace or a person's life. It's not good. What will it be like in eternity for those individuals to see a video replay of their life, complete with the thoughts they and those around them were thinking? Imagine their response when God shows them, "Here, here, and here were my warnings to you. Look how hard I tried to get your attention, but you refused to listen. What more could I have done?"

According to James 4:7, if we expose Satan and resist him, he will flee from us. But we have to expose and resist, not accommodate. Accommodation becomes treason, aiding and abetting the enemy. With this in mind, you may ask, "How much do I have to expose and resist? Do I have to go nuclear against my work colleagues when they are telling dirty jokes, using profane language, or passing around dirty pictures over email? Or do I get involved only when they are actually breaking the law?"

Chuck Missler of *Koinonia House Ministries* addresses this question quite effectively in his study of the book of Revelation, specifically Chapter 2:18–29, where the Apostle John recorded Jesus Christ's last message to the Church of Thyatira. This city, not too far from Ephesus, was the power center of Asia for the trade guilds of artisans and craftsmen. The trade workers from the Temple of Artemis, Paul's audience in the book of Ephesians, very likely belonged to these guilds. Because of the pagan and sometimes even occultist demon worship involved in these organizations, the Christian members would have had to decide for themselves how much they could accommodate the ritual practices that honored false gods.

The church of Thyatira had allowed the woman called Jezebel to infiltrate the church, teach false doctrine to the Christians, and lead them astray through the practice of eating food offered to idols. In his study of Revelation Chapter 2, Chuck Missler says that Jesus Christ reprimanded the church of Thyatira for not protesting these false practices. The church members likely didn't want to rock the boat, and decided to "go along to get along." Perhaps they were afraid of offending those who were coming to the church seeking a spiritual experience. In essence, because they didn't want conflict or were afraid to lose their jobs rather than stand for God's truth, they didn't confront this worship of false gods on enemy terrain, and allowed it to infiltrate and compromise their very own church.

Sound familiar?

In Revelation 2:24–25, the Lord encouraged those who had not followed her false teachings, "Hold on to what you have, until I come." He never told the individual artisans how much of these idolatrous practices they had to accommodate in their day jobs. He left this up to their individual consciences, as

Paul did in 1 Corinthians 11 and Romans 14. He expected them to hold on and not let go of the truth they possessed. He wanted them to pray and align themselves with His operational battle plans, the bigger picture of what He was doing in those places. But when the false doctrines got into the church, Jesus Christ and Paul strongly rebuked those who didn't resist Satan's schemes and expose the works of darkness.

Here's what this means to us: God has led you and me to a particular place, out there in the world, outside the safe perimeter of the church. He allows us to be confronted time and again by situations that go against His Word. What do we do? Do we let Satan deceive us into compromising our moral beliefs to maintain some pretense of unity or, at the other extreme, getting us to fight in anger, with fangs out and claws extended, in the power of our own flesh? Do we separate ourselves from our coworkers and have nothing to do with them? Do we muddle along, doing the bare minimum to keep our job and reduce the chance for conflict? Do we get out in front of the Lord's redeeming power and demand that our coworkers act like sanctified saints of God in our presence? Or do we train ourselves to submit to God's operational plan in wisdom and in love to shine His light, not our own, into the darkness? Do we align with His overall strategy of using the church to defeat Satan and rescue those trapped in his lies?

According to Ecclesiastes 3:1–8, there is a time and season for everything: a time of war and a time of peace, a time to act, and a time to wait. We find out the difference through our close walk with the Lord and through our alert and self-controlled exercise of bold faith and godly wisdom. The battle is God's, and it is His choice, not ours, when to employ escalation of force in His operational campaign. We need to be His willing instruments when He does so.

All of this assumes, however, that we are out there, in the world, getting up close and personal with those who do not believe as we do. God wants us to shine our light on the dark world, not only on each other inside the church.

A dear friend of mine who works in the full-time ministry recently confided to me that she has no close friends who are unbelievers. In fact, she said, she has no regular interaction with anyone who is not a Christian. How can this be?

Jesus told us to go into all the world and preach the gospel to every creature (Mark 16:15). There are many ways to do this. Jesus said in Matthew 5:15 and Luke 11:33 that we don't light a candle and hide it in a secret place or under a basket. Should we go into the nastiest, darkest places of sin, danger, and violence to shine our light? Maybe! We should be willing to do so if it's where God leads us. I know of a pastor who ministers to people working in the adult movie industry. He even rents a booth at their annual convention! Many Christians disagree with his approach to ministry, but this man carries out his mission, in the power of God, on the enemy's terrain.

Few Christians have the strength or maturity to withstand such a place of temptation and spiritual battle, but there are many people in those places whom Satan has taken captive. If we don't go out there to "find and fix" the enemy on his terrain, doing battle with him and shining the light of Christ into the darkness, these "prisoners of war" will be destroyed in their unbelief. If we don't stand our ground and hold on to the truths we have, Satan will infiltrate and compromise the church with these idolatrous practices.

In our ongoing battle with Satan, God expects us to be frontline warriors for Him no matter where He's placed us. We must prepare ourselves, training seriously and relentlessly to stand and resist in the decisive moment of contact with the enemy. In 2 Timothy 4:2, Paul encouraged Timothy to "be instant in season and out of season." We must take the high ground, own the terrain around us, make every effort to find and fix the enemy, and expose the works of darkness.

PRAYER: OUR FIELD OF BATTLE

A mighty Christian warrior may not necessarily have a strong physical presence. I know of a certain ministry where several frail great-grandmothers regularly meet in a building in upstate New York to conduct intercessory prayer. These elderly women storm the gates of the enemy and shake the powers of darkness to their core as awesome and mighty warriors of God. They're not afraid to get involved in the lives of others or to do battle with the devil in Jesus' name. Their close walk with God and their focused resistance to Satan's schemes serve as a critical force multiplier on God's battlefield. They know when to fight and how to invoke God's escalation of force as part of His purposes, not their own. They know it is impossible to be an effective warrior for Jesus Christ without a strong prayer life.

In Ephesians 6:18–20, Paul closed his landmark letter and discussion of spiritual armor by asking his audience to pray that he'd be bold in telling the gospel in the Roman prison.

He asked the same thing in Colossians 4:2–4:

Devote yourselves to prayer, being watchful and thankful.

And pray for us, too, that God may open a door for our message, so that we may proclaim the mystery of Christ, for which I am in chains.

Pray that I may proclaim it clearly, as I should.

Do you ever wonder why he didn't ask them to pray that God would get him out of jail?

In the same way Jesus prayed in the Garden of Gethsemane and went will-ingly to the cross, Paul knew he was in his Roman jail cell for a much bigger purpose in God's ultimate plan. He knew this wasn't about Paul himself. Rather, it was about God's plan for a whole bunch of other people: spreading the good news of Jesus Christ to the Gentiles across the Roman Empire. Paul could see the big picture because He had trained himself to walk closely with God in bold faith and godly wisdom. He knew God often works in strange ways that don't make sense to human wisdom. He knew God had stationed him in jail as a good soldier of the Lord Jesus Christ, manning an important outpost of light in enemy territory. He knew this was where God wanted him to shine light into the darkness. Rather than ask to be let out of jail, Paul asked for assistance from his fellow soldiers to band together in submission to God, and to each other (Ephesians 5:21), connecting with the angelic powers of the heavens to carry out God's will.

How important are our prayers to God?

We know He has chosen prayer as the means through which we make our requests known to Him. The Bible says in Matthew 6:8 that He knows what we'll ask before we do, and in Romans 8:26 that the Holy Spirit even helps us ask. So why does God want us to pray? Put simply, He loves to hear from us in this way: Proverbs 15:8 says the prayer of the upright is His delight. James 5:16 says the prayer of a righteous man is powerful and effective.

When we look closely at Ephesians 6:11-20, we see that prayer is where our spiritual weaponry clashes with the forces of darkness. Truth, righteous-ness, preparation, faith, hope of salvation, and the Word of God combine to expose the works of Satan and actively resist his efforts to deceive and destroy. These weapons align us with God's strategic and operational cam-paign plan that uses Christian believers of the New Testament church as His front-line warriors. Prayer is a focused act of communication and commun-ion with Him. It positions us to receive His specific mission orders, aligned with His Word and individually tailored to us. In military terms, we learn the "commander's intent" and pick up the battle rhythm of His operational campaign. We develop a deeper understanding of what He expects of us, and when, in His ultimate plan. In the ongoing battle against Satan, our prayers connect us with fellow believers and God's angelic forces that are at work all around us, fighting on our behalf in the spiritual realms. We likely won't physically see or fully understand this aspect of spiritual warfare until we reach eternity.

Let's look at the story of Jesus Christ in the Garden of Gethsemane. Notice what He asked, and did not ask, of His Father. During His life, Jesus often went alone to pray, receiving His mission orders and the Commander's intent. To help set the stage for this story, in Luke 10:17, Jesus Christ heard His disciples telling Him in amazement, "Lord, even the demons are subject to us!" Later, He took Peter, James, and John to the Mount of Transfiguration, where they saw Moses and Elijah appear with Him in His glorified form. Peter and the rest of the disciples had seen miracles and witnessed firsthand the power of God over Satan and his demon army. On the night before He was crucified, Jesus finished the Passover supper with His disciples and told them in advance that Judas Iscariot would betray Him. Then He went out to the Garden, again with Peter, James, and John. Kneeling there, Jesus agonized in prayer over God's will while they slept.

What happened next?

Judas arrived with a mob to arrest Jesus. Peter got excited, escalated force on his own and sliced off someone's ear with a sword. He had obviously forgotten how much power he'd seen through his association with the Master, or was ready to fight in his own flesh to bring in the Kingdom. In response, Jesus said, "Put away your sword. Don't you think I can call down twelve legions of angels if I need to?"

How many legions of soldiers were deployed throughout the Roman Empire at the time? Twelve! Jesus, had He wanted to, could have matched forces with the entire Roman army. He could have conducted some serious escalation of force of His own and turned everybody in that crowd into a smoldering pile of radioactive dirt. Surely that would have been a satisfying tactical victory, but it was not part of His operational mission in God's strategic plan. Jesus said as much in Matthew 26:54:

But how then would the Scriptures be fulfilled that say it must happen in this way?

Hebrews 12:2 (NASB) says, "[Jesus,] who for the joy set before Him endured the cross, despising the shame, and has sat down at the right hand of the throne of God." How did He know this was His mission? The answer is instructive for us. He was intimately familiar with the Scriptures that had predicted it, and He had just finished several hours of agonized prayer in the Garden. Sweating great drops of blood, He confirmed His mission orders from the Father. Then what happened? He got up and moved out to accomplish His orders with purpose, dedication, and endurance. Paul tells us in Philippians 2:5–10:

Your attitude should be the same as that of Christ Jesus: Who, being in very nature God, did not consider equality with God something to be grasped [held onto for personal advantage], but made himself nothing, taking the very nature of a servant, being made in human likeness.

And being found in appearance as a man, he humbled himself and became obedient to death—even death on a cross!

Therefore God exalted him to the highest place and gave him the name that is above every name, that at the name of Jesus every knee should bow, in heaven and on earth and under the earth.

Paul's telling us we should be like Jesus in our mindset toward the missions God gives us. We should know the Scriptures well enough to understand God's strategic and operational plan and the overall role we play in it. We should spend much time in individual and group prayer to get specific guidance as we execute our role as willing warriors through whom God carries out His ultimate plan.

We can make the case that Jesus Christ, on the cross, was Himself a major escalation of force in His Father's strategic plan. Three days later, God exercised the global nuclear option of all time. He completely and openly defeated Satan and his demons, making a public spectacle of the victory. Jesus understood the strategic plan, and His role in it, through His intimate walk with the Father. Several commentators observe that the incident in the Garden with the sword and the twelve legions of angels comment made quite an impression on Peter, who years later wrote in 1 Peter 3:12–14:

> *For the eyes of the Lord are on the righteous and his ears are attentive to their prayer, but the face of the Lord is against those who do evil.*

> *Who is going to harm you if you are eager to do good? But even if you should suffer for what is right, you are blessed. Do not fear what they fear; do not be frightened.*

Can you imagine Peter writing this letter and looking back across the years to that night in the Garden? In fear or anger, he lopped off the servant's ear with his sword and watched Jesus stick the ear back on his head. Peter remembered how Christ suffered for a much higher purpose than he, in his fleshly and unconverted state, could see that night. In 1 Peter 4:7, he encourages us to be aware of the bigger picture, when he says:

> *The end of all things is near. Therefore be clear minded and self-controlled so that you can pray.*

Peter learned firsthand how prayer prepared the Lord to be clear-minded and self-controlled as He was being led to His own death! He saw how an alert, disciplined, and intense prayer life develops a close walk with the God of the

Universe and enables Him to unfold His battle plan before us. Paul, in Romans 8:26–27, adds more insight:

In the same way, the Spirit helps us in our weakness. We do not know what we ought to pray for, but the Spirit himself intercedes for us with groans that words cannot express.

And he who searches our hearts knows the mind of the Spirit, because the Spirit intercedes for the saints in accordance with God's will.

Paul says in 1 Thessalonians 5:17 to pray without ceasing. What does this mean? One powerful example is told by Michael Catt, pastor of Sherwood Baptist Church in Albany, Georgia. Not long ago, Pastor Catt wrote a book called *Preparing for Rain*, in which he told how his church became a major influence in Christian films, producing the popular movies *Facing the Giants* and *Fireproof.* One thing struck me as I read the story: the church maintains a twenty-four-hour prayer chapel. Someone is on duty, standing watch—praying for the church and its film ministry, praying for the saints, praying for those who need Christ—all the time. Michael Catt and the movie producers, Alex and Steven Kendrick, strongly emphasize that their recent success in proclaiming the gospel through Hollywood-distributed films is due to this constant, intense, and focused prayer. It is part of an active, offensive, warrior mindset. Someone is in the chapel all the time, on patrol in the spiritual realms, actively shining light into dark places. The prayer warrior is in contact with the enemy and exposing his battle plans, escalating force in Jesus' name, and wreaking havoc in Satan's camp.

In today's world of Facebook, Twitter, cell phones, and text messages, we have an opportunity as never before to build a global prayer network of fellow believers in real time. Paul says in Ephesians 6:18, "And pray in the Spirit on all occasions with all kinds of prayers and requests. With this in mind, be alert and always keep on praying for all the saints." What power is waiting to be unleashed when the saints of God can unite in prayer at the same time, all over the world?

Paul said in 1 Timothy 6:12, "Fight the good fight of the faith. Take hold of the eternal life to which you were called." These words encourage us to be active and bold, not passive. If we, as warrior Christians, are on the offensive and teaming up in prayer, we can put the enemy on the defensive and expose the works of darkness with the armor of light through the gospel of the Lord Jesus Christ. We can get our missions from the Commander to physically go into those places that have been prepared through prayer. We can do this no matter where we are because, as Jesus said in Matthew 18:20, "For where two or three are gathered together in my name, there am I in the midst of them."

It is God's will that we pray and walk closely with Him. In response, He leads us through His Holy Spirit, in accordance with His revealed Word, to understand our mission orders, including when and how to escalate force in our immediate surroundings. Warrior Christians know that prayer is the way to unleash the power of God in this world.

FIRST TO GO, LAST TO KNOW

People who've served in the military are familiar with this saying:

First to go, last to know.

For years, warriors have said this to each other to express their somewhat jaded reaction when they receive orders to do a mission without being fully told what it is for or why they're doing it. Get on that plane or on that ship. Land at this place and accomplish this objective. *Why? What happens next? How long?*

Military personnel who are sent into the battle first are usually highly trained and can be counted on to deal with the extremely uncertain and intense situation that is sure to characterize the onset of combat operations. Something else is hidden in an expression like this. It is a code phrase among warriors that means, "I am part of a brotherhood. My fellow soldiers and I can handle whatever comes our way and come out on top. We're prepared to do the job even if we don't know much about it. We won't quit—we'll get it done."

The Bible contains many stories of people being told by God to do something without being told why. Most of the time, they followed through despite their doubts, fears, or lack of strength. Jonah, the reluctant Old Testament prophet, comes to mind. God told him to go to Nineveh, the capital of Assyria, to warn the people of imminent judgment. Instead, he headed off in the opposition direction. After a three-day encounter with a big fish, Jonah finally gave in and agreed to follow God's mission orders. He delivered the warning to Nineveh (which, interestingly, is present-day Mosul in Iraq). But something surprising happened. They repented of their evil and God spared them! For whatever reason, Jonah was not at all happy about this and stormed off by himself to have a pity party. God had to remind him that there are much bigger battles going on in His ultimate plan. He had chosen Jonah according to His purposes to be a specific part of it.

This concept of "first to go, last to know" has a huge bearing on how we determine and follow God's will. God decided to pluck Jonah out of his comfortable life and send him into enemy territory to tell the Assyrians they were toast if they didn't change their ways. The Assyrian religion, according to one story, predicted a messenger from their god would come from the ocean on a giant fish. God convinced Jonah, and the Assyrians, through some spectacular circumstances that He meant business. Jonah was the chosen person through whom He wanted to get the job done. Jonah couldn't understand why God chose him, why the Assyrians repented, and why all the hassle. But God had prepared Jonah, even taking into account his reluctance and initial rebellion, for this precise moment to save hundreds of thousands of people from destruction.

I believe we have the Bible story of Jonah and others like it to remind us how much God wants to use His children to accomplish His sovereign will. He could do it any way He wants, but He has chosen to use us.

From a certain viewpoint, God has clearly revealed His will for the rest of us. Yes, it's right there in the Bible. For example, in Isaiah 58:6-7, God asked the nation of Israel:

> "Is not this the kind of fasting I have chosen: to loose the chains of injustice and untie the cords of the yoke, to set the oppressed free and break every yoke?
>
> "Is it not to share your food with the hungry and to provide the poor wanderer with shelter— when you see the naked, to clothe him, and not to turn away from your own flesh and blood?"

Micah 6:8 says:

> He has showed you, O man, what is good. And what does the Lord require of you? To act justly and to love mercy and to walk humbly with your God.

Paul explicitly mentioned the will of God in several of his New Testament letters. For example, he said in Ephesians 5:17:

Therefore do not be foolish, but understand what the Lord's will is.

He admonished the Gentile trade workers in Ephesians 6:6:

Obey [employers] *not only to win their favor when their eye is on you, but like slaves of Christ, doing the will of God from your heart.*

Paul gave the Thessalonian church a list of things that constitute God's will. In 1 Thessalonians 4:3, he said:

It is God's will that you should be sanctified [set apart]: *that you should avoid sexual immorality;*

He followed with a more detailed list in 1 Thessalonians 5:14-22:

And we urge you, brothers, warn those who are idle, encourage the timid, help the weak, be patient with everyone.

Make sure that nobody pays back wrong for wrong, but always try to be kind to each other and to everyone else.

Be joyful always;

Pray continually;

Give thanks in all circumstances, **for this is God's will for you in Christ Jesus** [emphasis mine].

Do not put out the Spirit's fire;

Do not treat prophecies with contempt.

Test everything. Hold on to the good.

Avoid every kind of evil.

In Hebrews 10:36, he pointed out a significant aspect of God's will—perseverance:

You need to persevere so that when you have done the will of God, you will receive what he has promised.

James offered a well-known set of responsibilities for the believer in Jesus Christ. He said in James 1:27:

Religion that God our Father accepts as pure and faultless is this: to look after orphans and widows in their distress and to keep oneself from being polluted by the world.

Finally, Peter shared his own insights into God's will. 1 Peter 2:15 says:

For it is God's will that by doing good you should silence the ignorant talk of foolish men.

Think of the common themes these verses address. They tell us about certain behaviors and priorities God wants us to demonstrate in our lives. I think of them as essential skills for a warrior Christian, much as a soldier must know how to use his weapon and execute basic small unit tactics. Without these essentials, we can't prevail in contact with the enemy.

All elite warriors train hard. Their training makes them familiar with essential combat skills and confident in their ability to execute their assigned role in the larger campaign. God's training program for the Christian-as-warrior strengthens us in His power, enabling us to carry out His mission assignments, and giving us the courage to follow Him wherever He sends us. Take a look at Philippians 2:12 and 13:

Therefore, my dear friends, as you have always obeyed—not only in my presence, but now much more in my absence—continue to work out your salvation with fear and trembling,

For it is God who works in you to will and to act according to his good purpose.

Here is a clear description of the warrior mindset which can help us find and accomplish God's will. Paul said to "work out" our salvation. Was he saying our salvation is dependent on our works? No, it means something else entirely. The Greek word translated "work out" in Philippians 2:12 is from the root word *katergazomai*, which literally means "work down." It is also found in Ephesians 6:13, translated as "having done all," and James 1:3 as "develop." It conveys a sense of the rigorous training and physical conditioning a warrior must undergo to reach a high state of mission readiness. It is more like "working out" at the gym or, better yet, on a military obstacle course. To quote one more saying among warriors: "The more you sweat in training, the less you bleed in combat."

Chuck Holton wrote another book called *A More Elite Soldier* explaining the value of intense training for the Christian to be able to live on a championship level for Jesus Christ, to perform in "crunch time." A former Army Ranger, Chuck describes how members of elite military units endure incredibly difficult and challenging training programs so they can accomplish the missions given to them, no matter how undefined, chaotic, and dangerous they may be.

In Revelation 3:15, Jesus Christ told the lukewarm church of Laodicea: "I know your deeds, that you are neither cold nor hot; I wish that you were cold or hot." In verse 19 (KJV), he warns them, "As many as I love, I rebuke and chasten: be zealous therefore, and repent." The Greek words for "rebuke" and "chasten" relate more to training and discipline than to judgment or retribution. They describe a military drill instructor using a challenging training course to transform raw recruits into disciplined, skilled warriors. Anyone who has gone through boot camp understands what happens in this process: the recruits come in with priorities focused on themselves and not on the mission. The rigorous training program reverses those priorities.

Similarly, God brings us through difficult trials and experiences to align our own mental and spiritual priorities with His. This enables us to accomplish the challenging missions He wants to give us. But it happens only if we let Him. The word "zealous" in Revelation 3:19 means "earnest," or intensely serious. If going to be effective Christians-as-warriors, we must be intensely serious about submitting to His training program and aligning ourselves with His priorities.

When individual soldiers are assigned a mission, they may not fully understand the full scope of the military campaign in which they are participating. No, they are told to take this hill, capture that bridge, or ambush that enemy unit at this spot. Or, for that matter, fix this aircraft, cook this food, or process this paperwork. Every one of them must work together, accomplishing spectacular and mundane missions to defeat the enemy. When warriors have been trained to do their job, the commander expects them to submit to the mission order and carry it out well enough to accomplish the broader campaign objectives.

Another key point to consider about warriors and operational missions is this: sometimes, soldiers are not told to do something. They are asked. When I was in Iraq, our command center was near the Critical Surgical Hospital for the Al Anbar Province. Wounded Marines and soldiers were flown by helicopter directly from the battlefield to waiting teams of expert medical specialists who would provide them the urgent medical care they so desperately needed. These wounded warriors' chances of survival went up dramatically if they got to the hospital within a certain amount of time called "the golden hour." Whenever we heard the helicopters coming in, we knew what was going to happen next, and we prepared ourselves to respond. A voice would come over the loudspeakers that reached the entire base and would call out a certain blood type. The call meant that if you had that blood type, you shared it with a critically wounded soldier or Marine aboard the inbound helicopter, and he needed your help.

Now.

No one ordered you to give blood, but if you heard your blood type, you dropped everything and ran to the hospital as fast as you could go. By the time you got there, a line of other Marines and soldiers with the same blood type was already snaked around the building, each standing ready to donate his or her own blood. Everyone in line shared a bond with the wounded warrior, forged in common training experiences and in submission to a common mission. We shared a code of honor that essentially said, "I'd do it for you, because I know you'd do it for me." Our highest code of honor was that we would not consider letting down our buddies in the fight.

In much the same way, God, the Master Strategist, has chosen to engage you and me with Him in His several-thousand-year-long war against Satan. This is an intense, pitched battle taking place in the physical and spiritual realms for the souls of men and women all over the world. Casualties are coming in from all points of the compass. Prisoners are being held by the enemy, trapped and anxiously waiting to be rescued before they are annihilated. In the midst of this battle, God may not tell us to do something; He may ask us, because He knows we're part of His brotherhood and share His own code of honor. This code is summed up in the words Jesus said in John 15:13 (KJV):

Greater love hath no man than this, that a man lay down his life for his friends.

God wants us to be submitted to His mission and to our fellow Christians, ready to answer the call for help when it comes in. In most of the places where "submit" is used in the New Testament, the original Greek word is another military term meaning to "stand under," such as a soldier standing in formation. The word "submission" literally means being "under a mission." In military organizations, the commander says, "You have your orders," to which we in the Navy would respond, "Aye, aye, sir," and carry them out.

Today, Satan has deceived many Christians into thinking that a submissive person is a passive doormat, someone who's handed over his or her personality, goals, and decision-making abilities to someone else. He wants us to think that being submitted is allowing others to walk all over us. This misleading characterization has caused untold damage in the hearts of Christians and in church bodies. We must stand our ground against it.

According to the meaning of the original military-oriented Greek word, a submitted person is expected and encouraged to apply his or her own skills, talents, personality, and decision-making capabilities to the mission. General George Patton, in his World War II memoir *War as I Knew It*, gave the following advice to his military commanders: "Never tell men how to do something. Tell them what to do and let them surprise you with their ingenuity."

Marriage is undoubtedly the main place where this misunderstanding over the true meaning of submission causes so much trouble. Some people think, because the Bible says wives should be submitted to their husbands, only the man should be doing the thinking or making the decisions. Talk about a recipe for disaster!

The true meaning of submission should make us think of a man and a woman serving together on an important mission. They are obeying God and raising their children as a special operations team assigned to a forward outpost in enemy territory. The woman is "on board" with the mission, not fighting her husband at every turn nor turning off her brain so that the man can be completely in charge. The man is relying on the woman's wisdom, her perspective, and her complementary strengths to achieve better results than he'd achieve on his own. He's not doing his own thing and demanding blind obedience from her or ignoring her. A close look at Genesis 2 and Proverbs 31 should help clear up this one. God ordained men and women to work together in a marriage as a team, not as solo acts.

Remember the warning of James 1:16, "Don't be deceived!"

In 1 Corinthians 16:16 and Ephesians 5:12, Paul encourages Christian believers to submit to each other as we carry out God's mission orders. He stresses this point in Romans 12:10, "Be devoted to one another in brotherly love. Honor one another above yourselves."

Members of elite military units know intimately about honor. Pete Blaber, a former work colleague who commanded Army Delta Force units in Afghanistan and Iraq, summed it up well in the title of his book, *The Mission, The Men, and Me.* We're going to do what's right for the mission—that comes first. We're going to take care of our fellow warriors so we're all functioning at peak capability to accomplish the mission. "Me" comes last. Again, this is more about standing together in combat formation, aligned to a common mission, than about abdicating our own will and God-given abilities to someone else's personal dictates. As we carry out the mission, we need to consider how being submitted to God and to each other can help us stand our ground in the decisive moments of battle when we're in contact with the enemy.

The Christian-as-warrior perspective gives "the rest of us" insight into the spiritual battles raging around us and the weaponry available to us, so we can prevail against our determined enemy. We stand our ground against Satan and expose the works of darkness through the light of Jesus Christ we carry in our "jars of clay," our earthly bodies. We gain our mission orders through intimate prayer with our Commander. We team up with fellow Christians to carry out his battle plan. May we take these lessons to heart and emerge victorious as good soldiers of the Lord Jesus Christ.

THE RUNNER

Our second perspective of the victorious Christian life is of a runner competing to obtain a prize. Paul referred to it in 2 Timothy 2:5:

> *Similarly, if anyone competes as an athlete, he does not receive the victor's crown unless he competes according to the rules.*

Paul was apparently quite the avid sportsman. I can imagine if he were around today, he'd be in his jail cell watching *SportsCenter* on a big screen HDTV. He talked about athletic competition, running in particular, in most of his New Testament letters. He often used the runners of the ancient Greek Olympics to illustrate the Christian experience as one of purpose, discipline, and endurance. At the end of his life, Paul described his own journey as having been through a grueling training program and a difficult race, crossing the finish line to win the prize. The "Christian-as-runner" perspective shares many similarities with the warrior and highlights some interesting characteristics of God's will you may not have considered before. Given how often Paul talked about athletic training and competition, we certainly want to pay close attention to what he said.

COUCH POTATOES NEED NOT APPLY

Let's say you've been a couch potato all your life, and all of a sudden you feel like God is telling you, "I want you to run a marathon tomorrow!" You jump off the couch and shout, "Okay, Lord, I'll do it!" You quote Philippians 4:13, "I can do all things through Christ, who strengthens me." You put on your new running shoes and begin the race, running along in fine form, imagining what it will be like to cross the finish line and win the prize, crowd cheering, because, after all, God has called you, and you've heard time and again, "With God's calling comes God's enabling!"

But soon, your years of couch potato-hood and the laws of physics catch up to you, and you start to cramp up and find it harder to breathe. You keep running, more slowly, as your joints start to ache, your mouth becomes dry, and your feet start to blister. You're only at the two-mile mark and have twenty-four more miles to go. You're wheezing and puffing, your vision starts to blur, and your chest feels like it's going to explode. Your running stride degenerates into a waddle and then into a painful stagger. The couch-potato-turned-runner is now in such pain after a few miles that you have to quit the race.

You don't get the prize.

How many people do you know who felt "called of God" to do something only to quit when it became too hard? Is this the kind of experience God wants us to have? Big dreams and big calls unfulfilled, crashing to earth because of the ugly realities of life? Why do so many of us Christians expect a huge payoff with little preparation?

When I left the ministry and went back to college, I decided to major in electrical engineering because this program offered the highest starting salaries upon graduation of any program in the entire university. There was one problem: almost anyone could get in. With visions of big paychecks dancing in their heads, a couple of hundred students took the beginning *Intro to Double E* electrical engineering course each year. As they got deeper into the program, many prospective engineers would change their major to something a little easier (and offering a lower starting salary) or quit college altogether.

The electrical engineering program required about twenty-seven semester hours of advanced college-level math and at least as much chemistry, physics, and computer science. Many of the new students hadn't yet completed algebra or trigonometry, the high-school math courses that are a necessary foundation for engineering. They would have to take up to two years of remedial math just to get to the starting point of college-level calculus. Then they faced the fifty-plus hours of grueling math and science coursework before they got into an upper-division engineering class. I can remember only one classmate who made it to the senior year courses after starting with such a handicap. He pretty much had to be locked in a rubber room by the time he was done. Like running a marathon, the lack of proper training and preparation made this course of study incredibly difficult, and many people couldn't complete it.

This major was not for social butterflies. My engineering friends and I toiled away most nights in the computer lab, trying to debug some stubborn piece of software or make some electronic circuit work without frying the components. Meanwhile, many of our friends who had switched to other majors were partying or hanging out in the local bars, restaurants, and dance clubs. They laughed at us and told us how boring our lives were. Short-term pain for long-term gain was not something they were willing to endure. I have to tell you, on some days, pain was the only word that could describe our experience. Once we graduated, though, entire new vistas of opportunity were available to us "techies," including some well-paying jobs in Silicon Valley, because we had endured to the finish. On that note, I'm reminded of a rather gratifying quote from Scott Adams, the creator of the *Dilbert* comic strip: "Women don't want to date an engineer, but they'd like to marry one!"

Similarly, when I attended Bible college, I often heard young, eager Christians say, "God has called me to do such and such." But they weren't willing to get in shape to do it. We'd occasionally hear some blustery preacher ranting and raving:

"If God's called you to preach, get out there and preach!

"You don't need to be sitting in a Bible college learning how to parse Greek verbs; you need to be out there telling people about Jesus!"

In response, several of my young and impressionable classmates would quit school to start a church or work for some church and begin preaching. They would repeat the famous mantra, "With God's calling comes God's enabling," and plunge ahead. Unfortunately, they did not have the proper training and preparation, and lacked the strength to endure. They failed to acquire the knowledge and skills to run a church and deal with financial statements, payroll, budget planning meetings, deacons with hidden agendas, land purchases, government regulations, and legal contracts—the mundane, nitty-gritty essence of any enterprise they might have felt called to lead.

For whatever reason, many of these folks didn't want to take the time to prepare before they threw themselves into the race. They quit in discouragement. Some quit following the Lord entirely or spent years trying to overcome the bitterness and guilt of such a painful experience.

Training for the ministry, like a marathon, requires a level of commitment and focus that many of these people didn't have. In their emotional desire to follow the Lord's leading, they did not count the cost. In virtually every case I witnessed, these people looked for a shortcut to avoid the hard training and lessons that would prepare them for what would come their way. In essence, they bought a lottery ticket hoping for a big payout, and won nothing. They tried to run the marathon, but without the required preparation, they couldn't endure the rigors of the race.

THE RACE, SET BEFORE US

Hebrews 12:1 (KJV), one of the most often-quoted verses in the Bible, says:

> *Wherefore seeing we also are compassed about with so great a cloud of witnesses, let us lay aside every weight, and the sin which doth so easily beset us, and let us run with patience the race that is set before us.*

The Greek word translated "set before us," or "marked out for us" in the New International Version (NIV) literally means to "lie before." The image is of a public display lying in full view as an example for all to see. Paul says we are in a race God has laid in front of us like a public display. (Some Bible teachers don't believe Paul wrote the book of Hebrews, but I do. I believe the style, subject, and historical context all point to him.) How many of us can truly say that we see our whole race on display? Given all the books and sermons available on how to find God's will, it doesn't look like too many, does it? But what does our race look like from God's perspective? What perspective does an elderly person have, looking back on a lifetime of decisions and choices?

If you're like me, you're running your race one step at a time and see only one step ahead. You and I encounter all kinds of surprises, twists, and turns along the way. We navigate past obstacle after obstacle and wonder where we're actually going. Paul says *the race itself* is our opportunity to follow the Lord, persevere to the end, and win the prize. That opportunity, that challenge, is what God has laid before us on full display. As we saw from the book of Ephesians, God has ordained our role in the *ekklesia*, the church, which is His ultimate will for those of us living at this time in history. Next, God has ordained that we gain strength and wisdom through His training program made up of our life events, those obstacles and opportunities we encounter along the way.

In Hebrews 12:1, Paul tells us to run our race with perseverance or patience. The NIV translates the Greek word as endurance. He said nothing about style, speed, brute force, strong convictions or even a big smile on our face. He said to run with endurance. To be able to build endurance for a challenging race, we must train. Hard. We must, as Peter said in 1 Peter 1:13, "suit up and prepare for action." We must constantly test ourselves and measure our performance. If you're a runner like me, you can appreciate the connection between training, running, and testing. Paul clearly laid this out in 1 Corinthians 9:24–27, where he said:

Do you not know that in a race all the runners run, but only one gets the prize?

Run in such a way as to get the prize.

Everyone who competes in the games goes into strict training. They do it to get a crown that will not last; but we do it to get a crown that will last forever.

Therefore I do not run like a man running aimlessly; I do not fight like a man beating the air. No, I beat my body and make it my slave so that after I have preached to others, I myself will not be disqualified for the prize.

Paul reinforces the notion that the victorious Christian life is no couch-potato experience. He tells us to run our race with purpose, with a goal in mind, enduring to the finish to obtain the eternal prize. If we want to be part of the group of champion Christians to whom God will assign important and challenging missions, and the ones He will reward accordingly, we have to be in shape to perform at that level.

Why is this important? Think back to our discussion of the "call" one might receive from God to do a certain thing. Think of it in terms of the gifts, talents and circumstances described in Ephesians 4:7–16 rather than the vocation of Ephesians 4:1. If we as Christians are honestly seeking God's guidance and direction, and we get a strong sense from the Holy Spirit to pursue a particular goal, then several things should happen. This goal should be in accord with God's Word and affirmed through the wise counsel of others. Keep in mind, as I found out the hard way, we may sometimes have to sort through their true and hidden motives. The goal will likely take advantage of the individual gifts, talents, and circumstances we possess, but not always. Samuel went through all of Jesse's sons before he chose David to be king of Israel. If God is asking you to do something outside your skills and circumstances, I believe, He's going to make sure you know about it. We'll discuss this later, but His leading will never be contrary to His Word.

If all of these things are happening, then there is a responsibility to pursue this goal. It requires action and clear-headed thinking. God wants to see us endure and win the prize, which is the fulfillment of the course He has marked out for our lives. Jesus talked about this in Luke 14:25–35, a passage we saw in the last section. Here, he said to the big crowd following him:

> You can't be my disciple unless you love me far more than you do your family, are willing to leave them and pick up your cross and follow me.

> What person will build a tower without first counting the cost?

> What king will go to war without first determining whether he has the capability to fight the opposing army?

Jesus ended this talk by saying if a disciple quits before the finish line, he's like salt that has lost its savor and is put on the ground to be walked over by other people. Sure, it has a use, but not the one for which it was originally intended. This is different from the "bull's-eye" concept because it's not about missing the mark; it's about getting discouraged to the point of quitting. It's about getting sidetracked by a false idol. The great thing about God's will—and His grace—is if we miss the mark, we can try again. He wants us to. Using the illustration of a champion runner, Paul said in 1 Corinthians 9:26 that he does not run like a man running aimlessly. Running the race without preparation—or, at the other extreme, training endlessly without purpose—will not bring the prize. The prize comes only through intense training and getting into the race, running to win.

You might ask, "Why does it have to be this way for me? I've seen other people fall into a great opportunity merely by being in the right place at the right time. Why do I have to work so hard to find God's will?" I'd respond, "You don't see the whole picture. Do those other people actually have what they want? Is their easy opportunity a test from God to see how they'll handle it? All of us can count on the fact that at some point in our lives we will face obstacles and be tested." You might also ask, "What if God wants me to do this big thing now? Time is of the essence! I can't take more time to prepare!" I would ask if it's really God who is pushing you so quickly. Suppose God said, "I want you to run a marathon," would He want you to do it tomorrow before you're ready? As we saw in Luke 14, God doesn't expect His children to go on an important mission without preparation.

What if God had said to the couch potato, "I want you to run a marathon eighteen months from now"? Now, there's a different conversation with a different set of expectations. The couch potato has a measurable and manageable goal. He or she can do research, come up with a training plan, and build the necessary endurance to run and complete the race.

Anyone who has taken a course on time management or goal-setting might agree that the process of achieving a goal is fairly straightforward. There are literally hundreds of books, CDs, and seminars that tell us how to do it. We set the goal, break it down into manageable steps with timelines, and go to work, knocking off those manageable steps one by one. If we run into obstacles, we change our approach and find a way around, over, or through the obstacles to reach our goal. I used this approach for years when I worked as a project manager in the software industry.

You might ask, "Where is God in that? If the process of reaching a goal is so easy, why is the actual effort so difficult? Why can't God still do miracles? What about the stories of Him calling people, like David? He didn't look like much at first, but became a giant for Him. Goal-setting is something the secular world does!"

Think of it this way: would it be more of a miracle for God to just hand us everything we need along with a clear map of His will for our lives and a winning lottery ticket? How big a miracle is it to know He's using you and me, human beings making our own decisions on a daily basis to follow Him—or not—to accomplish His sovereign and ultimate plan? Is it more of a miracle that He's subjected each of us and His own plan to our physical and spiritual limitations, to the times in which we live, and to the way He's revealed Himself through His Word?

With this in mind, how do we get in shape to run our race and accomplish His plan?

GOD HAS A TRAINING PROGRAM?

When I was in Bible college, we set up an intramural volleyball competition every Friday night, made up of teams from all the dorms on campus. At first, our games were your typical church picnic "amateur hour" matches with no referee and few rules. The school decided to bring in a referee and develop a more formalized competition. For the first couple of weeks, we could barely serve the ball before the whistle blew. We hated it. Everyone was making mistakes and mishandling the ball. We couldn't stand the ref. After a while, we learned the rules and began to play volleyball the right way. The mistakes became fewer and the games became much more intense and exciting. We even started to like the ref! Because we were now playing the game according to the rules, we could compete at a higher level and enjoy it much more.

How does this story translate to our daily lives? How does God expect us to perform as champions in order to win the victor's crown of life? For years after I became a Christian, I couldn't help thinking God was angry with me, that He was fundamentally unhappy with who I was and what I was doing. Whenever things went badly or times became difficult, I thought He couldn't wait to punish me for wrongs I had committed against him, right things I forgot to do, or things I didn't realize I should be doing in the first place. I'll confess I brought a lot of guilt into my relationship with Christ, having been raised in a strongly performance-based religious denomination. Unfortunately, after I became a Christian, some people reinforced the notion that God was perpetually angry with His children for doing too many of the wrong things and not enough of the right ones. As a consequence, I lived for years in fear that I'd get struck by a bolt of lightning or that something bad would happen to me even though I was trying to stay out of trouble.

That's a heck of a way to live, isn't it?

I had to unlearn this whole outlook. I still have problems with it. It's taken a long time to grasp the fact that God isn't sitting up there in heaven, in a rocking chair with His arm raised, mad as He can be, and waiting to backhand me upside the head whenever I mess up. How many Christians live with this fearful view of God? It's important for "the rest of us" to realize our God is much stronger and much more in control than that. The Sovereign, Almighty God of the Universe judged our sins on the cross, made an investment in us with the blood of His own Son, and is now interested in training His children, you and me, to be like Him: righteous, godly, strong, wise, patient and full of His love. He wants us to succeed and to be in shape and strong enough to fully enjoy His blessings. Paul said in 2 Timothy 3:16–17:

All Scripture is God-breathed and is useful for teaching, rebuking, correcting and training in righteousness,

So that the man of God may be thoroughly equipped for every good work.

This passage uses words describing a training process used by champion athletic coaches. These coaches teach their athletes the winning techniques, *rebuking* or pointing out what the athletes are doing wrong, *correcting* or showing them how to do it the right way, and *training* them, or making them do it over and over until the techniques become second nature. At this point, the athletes are *thoroughly equipped* to compete effectively and deliver results. Paul is saying here that the Bible, God's Word, does the same for Christians. It is the most complete revelation of Him available to us today. It has come to us directly from His mouth, "God-breathed," and is profitable, useful, and beneficial for us to get in shape to accomplish His missions.

Living a life as a child of God in Jesus Christ is meant to be like living with the most wise, secure, and conscientious coach you could imagine. No mean, crotchety, and vindictive reprisals, but the calm, proactive teachings of a master mentor-coach who knows exactly what it takes to groom an athlete for championship performance. Similarly, parents know they can't do everything for their child—they have to teach the child so he or she can eventually do certain things on his or her own without help. Sometimes the teaching is difficult or even painful for the child. It doesn't change or diminish the love the parent has for the young one. The important thing is that the child learns. If we humans know this much, consider what Almighty God, our Father in Heaven, knows about training us to be champion Christians. He's not interested in humiliating us or beating us down in order to make a point. God doesn't need to make a point with us or anyone else. He made His point quite powerfully on the cross.

Some religions and a lot of Christian churches entirely miss this indispensable concept about God's complete victory over Satan. Why is this so? Why do we Christians often fail to take full advantage of learning from the Master, our Heavenly Father? As we saw in the last section, Satan's only effective tool against us is deception. He loves to twist our perception of God from the all-powerful, loving, and righteous Heavenly Father into a mean old buzzard. He will do anything to distort God's training program, designed to strengthen us and help us acquire His characteristics, into a series of retributions and punishments.

Recalling Paul's advice in 2 Timothy 2:5, "Similarly, if anyone competes as an athlete, he does not receive the victor's crown unless he competes according to the rules," we can appreciate how my college volleyball team learned to respect and value our referee's rebukes, correction and training. In Hebrews 12:5–12, Paul explains God's training program and describes how God gives us regular tests to increase our endurance. Like the exams we took in school, these tests measure our progress. They show us where we need to improve and let us see how far we've come.

You probably know Proverbs 3:5–6 by heart, "Trust in the Lord with all your heart and lean not on your own understanding; in all your ways acknowledge him, and he will make your paths straight." Do you know Proverbs 3:11–12? "My son, do not despise the Lord's discipline and do not resent his rebuke,

because the Lord disciplines those he loves, as a father the son he delights in."
The KJV says to not "be weary of His correction." Paul quotes these same
verses in Hebrews 12:5–6:

> And you have forgotten that word of encouragement that addresses you as sons:
> "My son, do not make light of the Lord's discipline, and do not lose heart when he
> rebukes you,

> Because the Lord disciplines those he loves, and he punishes everyone he accepts as
> a son."

The same words we saw in Revelation 3:19 are in this passage. They describe
an intense training program, not judgmental retribution. "Rebuke," as in 2
Timothy 3:16, is pointing out the difference between incorrect and correct
behavior. Our college volleyball referee "rebuked" us for several weeks by
blowing the whistle every time we did something wrong until we learned to
play according to the rules. "Discipline" is the reinforcement of habits that
produce higher-level championship behavior. My teammates and I "disciplined" ourselves to play volleyball the right way, practicing sets and volleys
again and again until we could do them right. "Punish" or "scourge" carries
the unfortunate notion of vengeance or vindictiveness. The Greek word literally means "whip" or "flog." In this case, it would be more like whipping
us into shape. While our referee didn't actually whip us, by the end of those
early games it sure felt like he had!

Next, in Hebrews 12:7, Paul says, "Endure hardship as discipline." In verse
10 he says, "Our fathers disciplined us for a little while as they thought best;
but God disciplines us for our good, that we may share in his holiness." This
is crucial to knowing God's will: He uses the hardships of life to discipline
us so we can share, or as the KJV says, "be partakers" in His holiness. This
isn't about working for salvation; it's about enjoying the fruits and blessings of
championship-level Christianity. It's about being in shape to endure the race
God has laid out before us and win the victor's crown.

The Marine Corps put out a recruiting poster a few years ago that showed a young recruit grimacing and struggling to make it over a difficult obstacle course. The caption under the photo said, "Pain is the sensation of weakness leaving the body." Compare this to Hebrews 12:11:

No discipline seems pleasant at the time, but painful.

Later on, however, it produces a harvest of righteousness and peace for those who have been trained by it.

The Greek word used here for "trained" is the same word from which we get "gymnasium." Paul is talking about God's "strength training program" for champion Christians. He emphasizes this point in Hebrews 12:12:

Therefore, strengthen your feeble arms and weak knees.

How's that for an intense strength training program? I can almost hear Paul, like a coach, yelling the cadence count as he leads us in pushups or deep knee-bends!

TRAINING FOR GODLINESS

Anyone who's participated in sports has a sense of what hard training is like: First, we have to *decide* we want to be part of the championship team and win the victor's crown. As Christians, this is deciding we're going to follow God's program and be serious about it.

Second, we have to *begin training.* This is about learning to walk with Him in prayer, reading His Word with purpose, seeing His hand in the things we do each day, and associating with as many other champion Christians as we can in order to learn from them.

Third, we have to *stick with the program*, using every day as a training opportunity and enduring with purpose. When things get tough, and we know they will, we have to keep our eye on the prize and follow the Lord, trusting Him as the Master Coach to lead the way as He strengthens us.

If we determine in our hearts to follow Him and not someone (or something) else, God will be the best coach we've ever known. He will take on the athletic trainer's responsibility of helping us to push ourselves a bit harder each day, expanding our limits and increasing our strength. Yes, it hurts at times because we're breaking through to a higher level of performance. In due course, we develop a much stronger relationship with Him through this training program and start to see more clearly what He's doing in our lives. We can then look back on the course we've run: a purposeful race that leads to the harvest of peace and righteousness of Hebrews 12:11. This harvest, which the KJV calls the "peaceable fruit of righteousness," is the alignment of our lives with His will, the strength of our conformity to Jesus Christ, the reflection of His character in us, and the blessings of partaking in His holiness.

Paul sheds more light on God's training program in his first letter to Timothy, his spiritual son. He says our training is a learning exercise with the expected outcome of *godliness*, the reflection of God's character in our lives. You may be familiar with 1 Timothy 4:7–8:

> *Have nothing to do with godless myths and old wives' tales; rather, train yourself to be godly.*

> *For physical training is of some ["little" in the KJV] value, but godliness has value for all things, holding promise for both the present life and the life to come.*

I've heard too many overweight Christians say, "Hey, the Bible tells me physical exercise is only of little value, so I think I'll pass up the workout and have another helping of dessert!" Thanks, folks, but Paul didn't say physical exercise or training was of no value. Why, then, is it worth only a little? Because no matter how good an athlete you or I may be, no matter how fit we are, we're still going to die someday. If we stay in shape, we might have fewer health problems later in life but our bodies will eventually give out. Paul's telling Timothy that godliness, on the other hand, has value in this life and the next.

Here's a key point: we don't have to wait until we get to heaven to fully enjoy the benefits of a godly life. If we train ourselves to a championship level of godliness in this life, we get to partake in God's holiness and His blessings here and now. Paul's basically telling Timothy, who is probably as big a sports fan as he is, that we need to train ourselves with the same focus and determination as those champion athletes of ancient Greece. They were required to train for at least a year, according to a strict regimen, before they could compete in the Olympic Games. We need to train for godliness. Paul uses the same Greek word for training ("exercise" in the KJV) he used in Hebrews 12:11, from which we get the word "gymnasium."

How do we train for godliness? Peter laid out the program for us. In 2 Peter 1:5–8, he provided his readers a detailed, methodical list of the steps we need to take:

> For this very reason, make every effort to add to your faith goodness; and to goodness, knowledge;
>
> And to knowledge, self-control; and to self-control, perseverance; and to perseverance, godliness;
>
> And to godliness, brotherly kindness; and to brotherly kindness, love.
>
> For if you possess these qualities in increasing measure, they will keep you from being ineffective and unproductive in your knowledge of our Lord Jesus Christ.

We don't get these qualities up front in some package deal with our transformed spirit (2 Corinthians 5:17) once we accept Christ. No, God's will is that we work at it and train for it. We must "make every effort" to add godliness to our faith and exercise ourselves to build it up. Note the sequence of what is gained—*goodness,* which is virtue or excellence in moral courage; *knowledge,* learning about God through His Word; and *self-control,* the same word Paul used in 1 Corinthians 9:25 for strict training or temperance. It means mastering our passions for a higher purpose. Next up is our favorite word, *perseverance,* the same one translated as endurance (or patience) in Hebrews 12:1. With endurance comes *godliness,* the reflection of God's character in us.

To this point, each attribute is internal to our own spiritual condition. Then comes *brotherly kindness,* meaning affection for fellow believers, and finally, *love,* which is the all-giving God-love Paul explains so thoroughly in 1 Corinthians 13. These last two traits are the outward manifestations of a built up, strengthened, and "in shape" spiritual condition of godliness. The letter of 1 John explains the depth of love found in the character and nature of God.

That love is reflected in us when we are submitted to Him in godliness. As John 13:35 says, "By this shall all know that you are my disciples, if you have love for one another."

God's training program for godliness is a continuous and parallel process. We don't wake up one day to find we have faith, moral courage, knowledge, self-control, or endurance. Look again at Peter's growth sequence. He said to "make every effort to add to your faith" these things. The literal meaning of this phrase is to "work as hard as you can to bring into play these things that supply your faith." Each characteristic we build up supplies and reinforces the previous one. The same word for "make every effort" is used in 2 Timothy 2:15, where Paul told Timothy to do his best, or work hard, to show himself approved to God. What's he talking about, especially when we're supposed to be saved by grace and not by works? Remember what Paul said in Philippians 2:12: he and Peter aren't telling us to work *for* our salvation, they're telling us to work *out* our salvation, to fortify our strength in Christ by building up the foundation of our faith with these godly characteristics. Peter explains this further in 2 Peter 1:3–4:

> *His divine power has given us everything we need for life and godliness through our knowledge of him who called us by his own glory and goodness.*

> *Through these he has given us his very great and precious promises, so that through them you may participate in the divine nature and escape the corruption in the world caused by evil desires.*

I don't know about you, but it seems I can barely make it through a day without hearing of another politician, pro athlete or business leader who sold his or her soul for money, power, or sex. We see wealthy people, who look like they have everything they need, agonizing about keeping up with their neighbors or compromising every ounce of their moral being to get more. We see others who, for whatever reason, did not grab the opportunities God placed in front of them. They have hardened their hearts with envy or bitterness because they don't have what someone else has. Peter says we can participate in the divine nature and escape the corruption of the world. In Hebrews 12:10, Paul says we can be partakers in His holiness by going through God's strength training program. To me, these two passages are like a big drink of cool water after a long, hot run! They are blessed promises to hold onto when we understand that God wants us *in* the race and not sitting on the sidelines.

Notice what Peter's not saying. We don't escape the world; we escape the corruption of the world. We don't have to get the filth of the world *in* us, even though it will likely get *on* us. Later, in 2 Peter 1:8, he says, "For if you possess these qualities in increasing measure, they will keep you from being ineffective and unproductive in your knowledge of our Lord Jesus Christ." I've known Christians who think that being godly means turning into some kind of fragile eggshell that breaks whenever a coworker utters a curse word or someone from the church commits a sin.

Satan has foisted another deception on the church that "God does not allow sin in His presence." What in the world does that mean? God didn't just allow sin in His presence; He went out and grabbed it by its miserable throat! According to 2 Corinthians 5:21, Jesus Christ, God in the flesh, was made sin. He jumped head-first into the nastiest part of the moral cesspool to fish us out and save us!

We are often told to be "in the world, but not of the world." Do we believe it? Jesus was sanctimoniously rebuked by the self-righteous Jewish Pharisees for hanging out with sinners. I can visualize these pious characters standing outside a burning building full of people trapped inside. Rather than rushing in for all they're worth to rescue the trapped people, they'd be standing around, leisurely debating some obscure aspect of the law and explaining why it would be wrong for them to get dirty, say, on a Tuesday morning before they've eaten lunch.

Godliness, the reflection of God's character, is being like Jesus Christ or David, who was called a man after God's own heart. Neither of them worried about getting dirty, which is different from getting corrupted. Let's be honest with ourselves. Our race is not a couple of gentlemanly laps around a track. It is an extreme competition where we'll crawl through mud, swing on a rope over shark-infested pools of water, fight off multiple opponents with swords, and carry wounded brothers and sisters on our backs over difficult obstacles to get to the finish line. Our race will stress the limits of our faith, push the edge of our endurance, and test the reflected character of God in us before we reach the end. There will be many times when everything around us and inside us is screaming, "Quit!" or worse, "Compromise!"

God has promised us that the time is coming when He will clean us up to stand with Him in blazing white robes on the victory podium to receive our victor's crown. But it's not going to happen if we're afraid to get in the race and get dirty, today! Peter and Paul encourage us: make every effort, work hard to become a champion. The more challenging the missions God gives us, the more we need this spiritual strength and endurance.

TRIALS, TESTS, AND TEMPTATIONS

James 1:2–4 offers strong words of encouragement to those of us who submit to God's strength training program:

Consider it pure joy, my brothers, whenever you face trials of many kinds

Because you know that the testing of your faith develops perseverance [the Greek word is translated as "patience" or "endurance" here and in Hebrews 12:1].

Perseverance must finish its work so that you may be mature and complete, not lacking anything.

Let's think about what he's saying: if you're getting body-slammed by the trials of life, well, you should count it as joy. If you're like me, your "not quite right light" is flashing bright red about now. How many people do you know who say, "Praise the Lord," when they're getting their head kicked in? Do they bug you—or scare you—as much as they do me?

My mom told me never to trust someone who smiles all the time.

So, what are we talking about here? It's basically this: we've been sold a bill of goods by Satan, and quite a few "prosperity gospel" ministers, that if things are going badly for us, we're doing something wrong. Now, I'm not talking about the consequences of sin. If you're reading this book and you're a Christian, hopefully you know full well that choosing to live your life in rebellion and disobedience to God denies you His blessings and intensifies the rebukes, correction, and punishment of His training program. We'll talk later in this section about what happens if we choose to follow an idol in the fleshly lusts of our heart.

I'm talking instead about what's going on when we're sincerely trying to follow Him and we're still getting hammered from all sides. In James 1:2, we are encouraged to look at the trials we "face" or, as the KJV translates more accurately, "fall into" as a *reason for gladness*. The same Greek word was used in Acts 27:41 to describe Paul's ship running aground on the island of Malta. In this case, it literally means "strike a reef with a ship." Jesus used the word to describe the Jewish man in Luke 10:30 who (KJV) "fell among thieves." Can you imagine James, as he wrote this verse, trying to find the right word to encourage believers who are suffering greatly for their faith? Imagine the Holy Spirit planting this word in his mind to hammer home the point: "Yes, from your standpoint it feels like you're getting your head kicked in through no fault of your own. But there is an eternal reason for it, and God is using it to make you strong."

According to James 1:3, the testing of our faith is designed to develop or build up (the same word used in Philippians 2:12 as "work out") our endurance. God does this, as James 1:4 says, to make us "mature and complete, not lacking anything." James used two different words for "complete" here to emphasize full development and peak condition. James is saying, "Make it a reason for gladness when you're smacking your head against life's obstacles, because God is using those seemingly random experiences to complete you and make you strong."

How's that for a picture of the Christian life?

From our perspective, these trials hit us unexpectedly and it's often difficult to see why. From God's perspective, they are planned with specific purpose. I'm reminded of the 1980s movie *The Karate Kid*. Young Daniel LaRusso is being taught karate by Mr. Miyagi, who begins by giving Daniel a bunch of chores: washing cars, sanding wooden floors, painting fences and walls. Mr. Miyagi tells him to do the chores in a specific way, but gives little guidance beyond that. After a few days of hard work, Daniel gets discouraged to the point of quitting. At the right moment, Mr. Miyagi shows him how the chores have actually conditioned his muscles to properly execute karate kicks and punches. They've enabled him to, in the words of Hebrews 12:10 and 2 Peter 1:4, "partake" in the discipline of karate. It's a breakthrough for Daniel, who forgets his frustration over the chores and now practices his punches, kicks and blocks with renewed purpose and *gladness*, according to the rules Mr. Miyagi has set down.

In the same way, our "chores," the random, minor hassles and heartbreaking tragedies of life blindside us as if we're striking a reef with our ship. They can discourage us to the point of quitting. From God's perspective, they have eternal purpose. They are training us to be champion Christians. They are building godliness in us so we can partake in the discipline of His holiness, in this life and the next. Think about elite athletes who belong to the top levels of their sport. How much more exclusive is a group of Christian believers who've achieved a peak level of spiritual strength and maturity?

How much more could we accomplish for God if we truly embraced this mindset? How much bolder could we be to press on through difficult situations and reach our goal? Paul said in 2 Timothy 1:7, "For God did not give us a spirit of timidity [or cowardice], but a spirit of power, of love and of self-discipline." God never intended for us to shrink from or be afraid of life's challenges, but to be trained and ready to handle them. Recognizing this, and accepting the purpose of God's training program, will help us focus our efforts and build up our spiritual strength to reflect His character.

Let's take another look at the Greek word *peirasmos* used in James 1:2 for "trials." It is also translated as "temptation" in James 1:13. Why does the Bible use the same word to describe God's strength-training program and Satan's attempts to compromise our effectiveness as Christians? When we are randomly blindsided by a difficult "trial," how can we tell if we're on the receiving end of a test from God or a temptation from Satan? The key is to use the same approach Jesus took when He was tempted by Satan in Matthew 4 and Luke 4. What did He do? He appealed to the Word of God.

The Bible is our rule book for the race we're in. It is our absolute benchmark of truth, the most complete revelation of God's will—and character—we have. Paul said we can't win the victor's crown unless we run according to the rules. How can we compete, much less win, if we don't know the rules? You can be sure our enemy knows them. He's using them against us all the time, trying to trip us up.

Have you played in a sports contest with someone who's always questioning the rules? I remember playing one-on-one basketball with a guy who pulled this stunt to try and beat me. He lied and cheated all through the game. Now, I'm no basketball star, so I am not sure why this was necessary. "You didn't do this; you were supposed to do that. You dribbled the ball with your hand on the side of the ball. That's carrying. You took two steps before you dribbled, that's traveling." We spent most of our time arguing about the rules of the game instead of playing. It was discouraging and I felt like quitting. Unfortunately, I didn't know the rules as well as I do now, and wasn't able to counter his tricks. It was a lesson learned: know the rules.

Questioning the rules is the oldest trick in Satan's book, starting with Eve in the Garden of Eden. Remember how he planted the seed of doubt in her mind? "Did God really say...?" If we aren't aware of what the Bible says, if we don't know God's rules and His promises, we become an easy target for Satan's lies and schemes. He will tell us we're facing difficult moments in life because we've let God down. He'll tell us it's not worth it to serve a mean and vindictive God.

How can we resist his lies if we don't know and master the truth of God's Word? Thinking back on Peter's process of training for godliness, the truth of God's Word reveals the essence of God's character He wants us to reflect in our own lives. Beth Moore wrote a timely and relevant book a few years ago called *When Godly People Do Ungodly Things*. Her book discusses how people in high-profile positions of ministry sometimes end up committing extremely visible and damaging sin. Beth talks about how Satan constantly probes the perimeter fence of our heart, looking for a weak fencepost he can wiggle back and forth to make a hole big enough to squeeze through. Soon enough, he's wormed his way inside and is devouring our most precious assets. She quotes Proverbs 4:23, "Above all else, guard your heart, for it is the wellspring of life." Guard your heart! Beth Moore encourages us to watch those fences around our hearts and maintain them in good repair to keep Satan out.

If you've been a Christian for any length of time, you know how this works. You see something very attractive in front of you—a good-looking, charming person, a bunch of money, a fun time. Adventure. Companionship. Revenge. A new, "cool" religious doctrine or practice—Satan transformed into an angel of light. It looks innocent enough, and you think, *Surely this isn't going to hurt anyone. No one will ever know.* But someone does know. Satan knows your weaknesses, and God knows your heart. Here is the decisive moment with the enemy: you either lower your guard or you do not.

James 1:12–16 examines this in detail:

> *Blessed is the man who perseveres under trial, because when he has stood the test, he will receive the crown of life that God has promised to those who love him.*
>
> *When tempted, no one should say, "God is tempting me." For God cannot be tempted by evil, nor does he tempt anyone; but each one is tempted when, by his own evil desire, he is dragged away and enticed. Then, after desire has conceived, it gives birth to sin; and sin, when it is full-grown, gives birth to death.*
>
> *Don't be deceived, my dear brothers.*

The familiar Greek word *peirasmos* is translated in verse 12 as "trial" and in verse 13 as "tempted." Don't these two verses have entirely different meanings? Yes, they do. And there's another twist: the word for "test" in verse 12 is a different one, *dokimos*, which means "prove." Taken together, these verses tell us that God allows us to be *tempted* by Satan as a *trial* in order to learn to resist his evil schemes, build endurance, pass the *test* and *prove* ourselves as victorious, champion Christians.

Anticipating what a few people might think when they read this passage, James immediately responded: "Some of you are now going to turn around and blame your sin on God. 'Well, He tempted me,' or 'God allowed me to be tempted.'" Not so. If we yield to the temptation to sin, according to James 1:13, it's because we've allowed ourselves to be dragged away through our own sin nature and our own lusts, and enticed to sin. The Greek words for "dragged away" and "enticed," according to Bible commentator Warren Wiersbe, are hunting terms that describe being lured into a trap with bait. We see something attractive and, because of our own fleshly desires, choose to go after it.

While God uses these trials and tests to strengthen us as champion Christian runners, Satan uses them to try to cheat us out of our prize. You may say, "Well, Tom, this doesn't sound too fun. What if I'm not strong enough to pass the test?" Paul gave us a comforting promise in 1 Corinthians 10:13:

> *No temptation* [there's the word *peirasmos* again] *has seized you except what is common to man. And God is faithful; he will not let you be tempted beyond what you can bear. But when you are tempted, he will also provide a way out so that you can stand up under it.*

Even though the trials, tests, and temptations hit us hard as if we're striking a reef, the fact remains that God is aware of the entire process and every event that comes our way. God, like the master coach, lines up these trials and tests as training events to specifically prepare us for greater, more challenging missions He wants us to complete. He's not going to push us harder than we're capable, even though, like a good coach, He may push us harder than we think we're capable.

RABBITS, TURTLES, AND FROGS

Consider two verses from Proverbs highlighting a couple of human traits that can trip us up as we run our race:

> Proverbs 28:20: *A faithful man will be richly blessed, but one eager to get rich will not go unpunished.*

> Proverbs 21:25 (KJV): *The desire of the slothful killeth him; for his hands refuse to labour.*

These verses remind me of some well-known stories about rabbits, turtles, and frogs. The first story is about a rabbit in a race with a turtle. The rabbit takes off running while the turtle plods along. Sure enough, the rabbit gets distracted and wanders off the track, losing the race to the slow but steadfast turtle. You probably know people who are like rabbits. They're into all kinds of things, running from place to place, busy as they can be, yakking away on their cell phones, text-messaging, multitasking while on vacation, and leading conference calls while picking up the kids from soccer practice. You wonder if they ever finish any of the projects they start. This is familiar territory for me. Except for the part about picking up the kids, it pretty accurately describes me. I've got ten projects going at any one time. I can barely sit through a TV show anymore unless I have a book in my lap and am checking my email or reading the *Wall Street Journal* from my smart phone.

With all of the choices available today, you and I could take up every minute of our day with some type of "spiritual" activity. Many churches fill their calendars, and their parking lots, with program after program. How many of us spend as much time as we can inside the church building, busying ourselves with studies, workshops, devotionals, prayer groups, and so on? Are we taking this knowledge back into the world to the people who need it? Or are we like the boxer and runner Paul describes in 1 Corinthians 9:26, beating the air and running aimlessly through our continual reading, listening, and note-taking?

Similarly, we see in Acts 16 how Paul and his group made plans to go into various regions of the Roman Empire and how the Spirit of God stopped them. Like them, I'm always probing and prodding God, asking, "Lord, is it time to move yet?" Kathy and I get antsy when we've lived in a house for two years. If I'm in a particular job longer than that, I feel like I'm stagnating. Gotta keep moving! It has been a long struggle to learn to slow down and not get ahead of God. I've tried many times to find a new job, get a transfer or promotion, or move to another city to keep from getting bored. At several points in my life, God has visibly and loudly slammed doors shut to keep me in a particular place so He could teach me and bless me.

A familiar Old Testament verse is Isaiah 40:31:

> *But they that wait upon the Lord shall renew their strength; they shall mount up with wings as eagles; they shall run, and not be weary; and they shall walk, and not faint.*

The Greek word used for "wait" in the Septuagint translation of this verse is from the same word for "endurance" we've seen in Hebrews 12:1, 2 Peter 1:6 and James 1:2. Here's something you may not have heard too often: "Waiting on the Lord" is not sitting in a chair, looking at your watch, and tapping your fingers on the table until God shows up. No, it is enduring, powering through your current circumstances, staying close to Him, and claiming His promises until He changes your situation or leads you somewhere else.

You may be familiar with the story in Luke 10:38-42 about Martha and Mary, the two sisters who hosted Jesus in their home when He passed through their village. Martha was busy working and preparing everything for His stay, while Mary was sitting at His feet listening to Him talk, taking in every word.

Martha got upset and asked Him why He didn't care that Mary was, as she saw it, lounging around and yakking away. Jesus told Martha that Mary had "chosen the better part." He probably told her He didn't care if the potato chips and *hors d'oeuvres* were arranged on the food tray just so; He was there for the spiritual fellowship with good friends.

I think of this story every now and then, especially when I'm stuck at a long stoplight. I pray, "Come on, Lord, I'm trying to be a good steward. I've got all these things going on, and for crying out loud, I'm growing old sitting here at this light." He gently reminds me about Mary and Martha. Proverbs 21:5 also comes to mind: "The plans of the diligent lead to profit as surely as haste leads to poverty." I can almost hear the Lord saying to me, "Come on, Tom, don't try to boil the ocean. Step back and focus on what's important. Walk with me. I will lead you if you'll let me, and oh, by the way, I know exactly how long this stoplight will be red."

Ouch.

There's another story about a frog sitting in a pot of water. When the heat under the pot is slowly turned up, the frog sits there until it's boiled to death. It stays, trying to adjust to its environment, no matter how hot it gets. The frog needs an unmistakable prodding from the outside in order to move.

I know too many people like this. They aren't going to move unless they get smacked with a two-by-four that has the words "GET OUT" stenciled on the side. Changing jobs, taking on a new opportunity, learning a new skill, moving out of their comfort zone—anything that forces them to change their current routine is difficult. Not to be too harsh, but they make me think of Proverbs 22:13:

> *The lazy person is full of excuses, saying, "If I go outside, I might meet a lion in the street and be killed!"*

Sure, that's possible, but not likely. The frog always has an excuse to avoid change, to not get out of the soon-to-be-boiling pot. A bestselling business book talks about this very thing. *Who Moved My Cheese,* by Spencer Johnson, M.D., came out a few years ago and was an immediate hit with corporate managers. A short book with big print, it seemed like Dr. Johnson wrote it with a crayon so all of us rabbits, the busy multitasking road warriors who have no attention span and a million things to do, could read the whole thing on a short airplane flight.

The story is about two mice that go through a maze each day to find a piece of cheese. One day the cheese is not there. One mouse sits in its usual spot, waiting for the cheese to be delivered. It never shows, and the mouse dies of starvation. The other, more enterprising mouse goes back into the maze to find more cheese. This little book was written to encourage people in the business world to anticipate change, to not get overtaken by events or get stuck in a rut. I saw this all the time in the software industry—the most difficult thing we could do was get our customers to embrace change, even when they could see their current business model crumbling around them.

How do we know the right balance, from God's standpoint, to avoid being a rabbit without becoming a frog, and vice versa? We can easily find verses in the Bible to support either position. Many times, we rabbits want to move from our present situation because of pride. *I'm not making enough money in this job. Nobody here appreciates me. I can do better than this.* We convince ourselves we belong someplace better. We may believe those around us don't deserve our talents and full effort. *I don't want to waste my time with these people. If I could get that other job, I could afford that nice house or new car.* How many times do we rabbits get out in front of God and leave early, giving up the opportunity to minister to those around us or to have God take us through a valuable training lesson? How many times have we given up a bigger blessing we couldn't see at the time in order to grab a smaller one we could see?

For the frogs among us, the reluctance to change, or to even get in the race, can come from a lack of faith that is rooted in fear. Perhaps a bad experience in the past hurt you deeply. *I'm never going down that road again.* Maybe it's a feeling you'll let someone down if you leave your current post. You see all the signs warning you to get out, but you can't get off the dime and make the move. Or, maybe it's because you've had one too many "do-overs," where God wraps the same opportunity or test in a different set of circumstances, making us go through it again so we might learn the lesson He's trying to teach us. The frogs may sigh to God, "Lord, I'm tired. I don't feel like going through this again."

Picture a runner who has completed a difficult training workout. With legs burning and chest bursting, this athlete feels like he or she can't do any more. "Just one more lap!" the coach yells. The runner musters all of his or her strength and does one more. There's a breakthrough. He or she now knows there's a reserve of strength to draw on and do more than was previously possible. Proverbs 10:9 says, "The man of integrity walks securely, but he who takes crooked paths will be found out." My older brother once told me something similar, "There are no shortcuts; everyone eventually pays his or her dues."

For rabbits and frogs alike, laziness or unwillingness to pay our dues can be a huge issue. The rabbits don't want to take the time. The frogs don't want to take the risks.

We have to get out of our comfort zone and submit to God's training program—on His timetable.

TALENT, LUCK, OR PREPARATION?

My older brother said something else to me a few years ago during the Internet dot.com boom that stuck with me:

Don't stand under a waterfall and call yourself a rainmaker.

He was talking about some of the people in the software industry with whom he and I worked. They were landing huge sales deals, receiving promotions every six months, and becoming senior executives of hot Internet companies while they were still in their late twenties or early thirties. These people were convinced that their success was due to their incredible "rainmaking" sales skills, a top-ten-MBA-program education, or hard-nosed business acumen. In retrospect, it was due to historically favorable market conditions where it seemed almost anyone could sell anything software-related.

One of my old bosses, a senior vice-president, in an unexpected moment of candor, told me a monkey could have sat in his chair and the company would still have made money. Worse, several senior executives at the company where my brother worked were found to be fabricating an elaborate series of fictitious business transactions. They were sent to prison and the company no longer exists.

When the economic bust came and so many businesses went under, it became clear that success in the good times was not a reliable indicator of true managerial ability. Many of these people were unable to execute their business models or keep the money coming in during the lean times. In too many cases, they laid off the real workers and kept their cronies and friends. When the business picked up, the friends didn't know how to capitalize on the market conditions. It was a tough time to learn if they had the skills and wisdom to sustain their companies.

Proverbs 24:10 (KJV) says, "If thou faint in the day of adversity, thy strength is small." The difficult times, not the easy times, are the true measure of our strength and character. This applies as well to the Christian race marked out before us. Let's not kid ourselves: real, championship-level spiritual maturity isn't standing under a waterfall and calling it rain. We can't think, for example, because we have a laid-back temperament or aren't tempted by some of the more "visible" sins, we are truly wise or spiritually mature. We must be cautious of calling ourselves strong and committed believers if we're living and working in the safe confines of a church where, like my Bible college friend, we don't even know any people who aren't Christians.

Some people possess great talent and make life's challenges look easy. There was a guy on our high school track team who used drugs and partied all the time, usually coming to practice half-stoned out of his mind. He'd goof off in practice, go to the track meets, win the races, and easily smoke the competition. As a 400-meter guy, he ran this punishing race in under forty-eight seconds, while the rest of us had to practically sweat blood to break fifty seconds. He did great for a while, but the drugs and hard living caught up with him and he quit the team. The rest of us got little benefit from his natural abilities. A lot of talent went to waste.

You may have seen the movie *Rudy,* the inspirational story of Daniel Ruettiger, a not-so-gifted athlete who made the University of Notre Dame football team in the 1970s as a walk-on and eventually played in a National Collegiate Athletic Association Division I game. Rudy lacked talent and physical size, but more than made up for it with heart and tenacity. There's a scene in the movie where Notre Dame coach Ara Parseghian tells him that he wishes he could put Rudy's heart in some of the other players' bodies. This undersized and dyslexic dreamer persevered through all kinds of hardships to play in only one game.

The movie has been a favorite for years. As John Eldredge would say in his book *Waking the Dead*, Rudy's story resonates deeply within us, another story God has written on our hearts. It is the story of persevering against the odds, of working hard to overcome the obstacles to win the victor's crown. Paul encourages us to realize this story in our own lives. In Hebrews 12:1, he says, "Run the race with endurance," and in 1 Corinthians 9:24, "Run to win!"

Although they are not the same things, intense preparation and endurance can often look like natural talent, even luck, to outsiders. In Acts 18, Paul appeared before Gallio, the Roman *proconsul*, or military governor of Greece. Gallio's younger brother, Lucius Annaeus Seneca, was a Stoic philosopher. Known today as Seneca the Younger, he coined a phrase that endures to our time:

Luck is what happens when preparation meets opportunity.

Another movie favorite, called *Miracle*, is based on the true story of the 1980 U.S. Olympic hockey team. This team of amateur players beat the near-invincible Soviet Union team and eventually won the gold medal for the first time in twenty years. The American coach, Herb Brooks, did not pick the best amateur players to be on the team. He picked the players who would make the best team. In one scene of the movie, the coach reminds the Olympic Committee that championship teams are rarely made of all-stars. All-stars are individual performers, Coach Brooks said, and he needed an exceptional *team* performance to beat the Soviets. He had less than a year to prepare them to go against a team that had been together for over a decade. What might have looked like luck in the pivotal game was true endurance and desire, cultivated by hard work that shaped the team into championship excellence. For months, Herb Brooks worked this team incredibly hard. When the opportunity came, they were prepared. They were able to endure through the grueling contest and seize the moment late in the game to score and beat the Soviets. Their victory electrified a nation and still inspires many thirty years later.

Let me ask you this: what is your dream? What vision has God laid on your heart? What do you think about at two o'clock in the morning, when no one else is around? What is the sense of urgency you feel inside, calling out to you alone? When you stand before God, how will you answer Him for the dream He's given you? How badly did you want it? Did you nurture it in prayer and obedience? How did you prepare yourself to meet His challenge to you and stick with it through tough times? Using Paul's words from 1 Corinthians 9:24-27, are you running with purpose or are you allowing yourself to be an aimless Christian couch potato who will be cheated out of the victor's crown?

AVOIDING DISQUALIFICATION

In 1 Corinthians 9:26, Paul said he didn't run aimlessly or swing his fists in the air. Instead, he said in verse 27:

No, I beat my body and make it my slave so that after I have preached to others, I myself will not be disqualified for the prize.

Now, why would Paul, of all people, write this? He was deadly serious, and it's scary to consider how easy he thought it might be to lose the prize. This came from the premier apostle of the New Testament, God's missionary to the Gentiles of the Roman world. I heard a radio preacher say that Paul was the second greatest man who ever lived, next to the Lord Jesus Christ Himself. In the first few verses of 1 Corinthians 9, Paul had to remind the Corinthians of his apostolic authority. Corinth was a "carnal" church, and he was dealing with several serious issues regarding their commitment to a godly lifestyle. His letter was pretty hard on them. Why would he, in the middle of this, so explicitly point the finger back at himself?

Paul was not talking about losing his salvation, mind you. As he said in many places, such as Ephesians 1:7 and 1:13–14, our salvation is guaranteed by the blood of Christ and the presence of the Holy Spirit within us is our down payment of redemption. Rather, Paul's concern was about his *reward*: running the race according to the rules of God's training program so he wouldn't be disqualified from the victor's crown at the finish line. He fully expected to be in heaven with the Lord, but for some reason was concerned that he would not reap the benefits of a lifetime of service to Him. Why?

The Corinthian church members would have fully understood Paul's sports-oriented terms in verse 9:27 due to the importance and popularity of the

Isthmian Games. These Greek games were held in Corinth during the off-years of the ancient Olympics, like today's Asian or Pan-American Games. Several commentators have noted his use of the Greek word *keruxas*, meaning "herald," that is translated "preached" in this verse. At the end of a race in the Greek Games, a herald or announcer would proclaim the winner and single out anyone who had been disqualified from the race. This would happen because they'd cheated during the race or had failed to observe the prescribed year-long training regimen. The word for "disqualified" is *adokimos*, literally to be "not proven," or "not meeting the test." This adds another dimension to James 1:12-13 and his treatment of the words "test," "trial," and "prove." Paul emphasized that he worked hard to avoid failing to meet the test or, in the words of 2 Timothy 2:5, not having competed according to the rules.

How can someone be disqualified from the Christian race or fail to meet the test? Paul answered this question in 1 Corinthians 10 with the well-known story about the Old Testament Israelites wandering through the desert for forty years. The children of Israel, having passed through the Red Sea, were following the cloud God provided by day and the pillar of fire by night. He used these phenomena to guide them in their travels away from the slavery of Egypt. He gave them manna and quail to eat, and they drank water from the "spiritual rock" (1 Corinthians 10:4). Then what happened? In verse 5, Paul said that God was not pleased with them and scattered their bones all over the desert wilderness. In verse 6, Paul tells us this was done for our example so we wouldn't do the same evil they did.

What did they do that was so wrong?

Though they experienced firsthand God's miraculous deliverance and His daily provisions, apparently it wasn't good enough for the children of Israel. In 1 Corinthians 10:6–10, Paul tells us what they did wrong:

Verse 6, they set their hearts on evil things;

Verse 7, they were idolaters;

Verse 8, they practiced sexual immorality;

Verse 9, they tested the Lord;

Verse 10, they grumbled against Him.

These five sins have something in common: they are all indicators of idolatry (verse 7), which is the desire to follow and worship someone or something other than the true God. Psalm 78:18–20 describes in greater detail the hard-hearted, ungrateful attitude the children of Israel showed toward God after they left Egypt:

They willfully put God to the test by demanding the food they craved.

They spoke against God, saying, "Can God spread a table in the desert? When he [Moses] struck the rock, water gushed out, and streams flowed abundantly. But can he also give us food? Can he supply meat for his people?"

Did you notice the word "test" ("tempt" in the KJV) in these passages? Yes, it's the same Greek word *pereismos* we've seen before. Here, it is a huge no-no. The children of Israel were testing God, putting Him through a trial with (in their minds) an uncertain outcome. They were telling Him they knew more about their circumstances than He. In the face of God's continuing deliverance and the dramatic revelations of His power, the "stiff-necked" children of Israel provoked Him again and again by questioning His ability to provide for them and by second-guessing His motives. Imagine: God had just miraculously delivered them from Egypt, including a walk down a dry path in the middle of the Red Sea and the destruction of the Egyptian army, and now they doubted He could provide food. "Would to God we had died by the hand of the LORD in the land of Egypt, when we sat by the flesh pots, and when we did eat bread to the full," they complained (Exodus 16:3, KJV). As soon as Moses went up to Mount Sinai to commune with God, the people engaged in sexual immorality and made an idol, a golden calf they could worship instead of the true God. It's no wonder He scattered their bones across the desert.

These people had not bought into God's plan for their lives, at all. Using this story as an example, Paul warned the carnal Corinthians of the same real danger they faced. They were abusing their liberty in Christ for selfish reasons, hardening their hearts against God and turning toward idols, practicing sexual sin and grumbling against Him. Paul gave a similar warning to his audience in Hebrews 3:8: "Do not harden your heart, as you [the children of Israel] did in the rebellion."

You might ask, "How does this apply to my life today? I'm not hardening my heart, worshipping false gods, engaging in open, immoral sex, or grumbling against God." The list of sins from 1 Corinthians 10 are probably more subtle in practice among Christians today than they were in Paul's or Moses' time, but will bring about the same results. A greater danger faces those who think they are following God but have their heart focused on something else. Think for a moment about the priests and rulers of Israel who lived in Jesus' day. In Matthew 6, Jesus pointed out the corrupt religious leaders who would pray, give money, and preach in their own spiritual pride to be seen and admired by others. Jesus said of them, "They have their reward." In their zeal to obey the Law, and in their spiritual pride, they completely missed *Ha'Mashiach Nagid* of Daniel 9:25, the Anointed One of Israel, when He was literally standing in their presence! In their desire to worship their own religion, they killed Him.

Paul's warning is as strong today as it was in the time of those Corinthian Christians who continued to dabble in pagan idol worship. We still face the dangers involved in following religious practices, or religious liberties, rather than following the Lord. Satan sneaks in with his lies about religion and worship to get us off track. He loves to use our pride and our zeal to take our focus off God's missions and training program. When I was in the corporate world, I often noticed people coming into the workplace with a zeal for the gospel. Wearing their faith on their sleeve, they would hold Bible studies during lunch and actively participate on the Christian email lists in our company. Over time, however, it became evident that their heart was set on something other than God. Their zeal appeared to be for appearances' sake. They seemed more interested in exercising control over others or following some preacher or doctrinal position. Rather than submitting to and following God's plan for the corporate environment in which He'd placed them, it seemed they were trying to "rack up souls" for the Kingdom or establish a platform for a particular doctrine. Too often, they showed little apparent concern for how, or whether, the Spirit of God was working in the lives of those around them.

You probably know people who are quite caught up in their personal holiness, adhering to the "do's and don'ts" of Scripture and commanding everyone around them to do the same. This described me at one point in my life. All too often their hearts are very cold, to the point that they saddle a person in need with a whole slew of demands before they will offer any real help. Some churches post a dress code on their front door, keeping out anyone who doesn't conform. Like the Pharisees, they'd likely criticize Jesus Himself for hanging out with and helping sinners.

Other people are so caught up in the idea of Christian liberty that they'll purposely and carelessly do things without regard for the impact they might have on the spiritual morale of others. I'm guilty of this as well, far more often than I care to admit. In his letter to the Romans, Paul brought this up in the context of people eating meals that had been sacrificed to pagan, demon gods. He made the point in Romans 14:12 that if it caused someone to stumble, he wouldn't do it. Now, there's a limit to this kind of thinking because I've seen other Christians use this verse as a hammer to control or intimidate others. My former pastor quit chewing gum because someone had told him he found it offensive. Isn't that carrying it a bit too far?

Here's the principle Jesus brought up: if we go through the motions of serving God for reasons other than honoring and glorifying Him, and following Him wherever He chooses to lead us, we will get the fleshly reward which those actions bring in this life. At the same time, we will forego the eternal victor's crown that could have been ours.

There's a more dangerous possibility to consider. Jude, the brother of our Lord, wrote a short New Testament letter to warn about evil men who had snuck into the church to push their own fleshly agenda. These men, similar to the children of Israel, were grumbling against God, following their own wisdom and even mocking Him. In doing so, they invited His judgment upon themselves and those around them. How many pastors and religious leaders, not to mention people in the pews, focus on theological viewpoints or aspects of church doctrine to the point of worshipping those topics rather than the Lord Himself? Jude's warning to us is to be wary of those who circulate among Christians but do not have Christ in their heart. They are following their own passions and lusts, and are using the things of the Lord solely to further their own fleshly interests.

It's critical that we remain, as Peter said, sober and vigilant against these sneak attacks from Satan. Grumbling and murmuring come into play when someone is not interested in God's answer, only in holding on to what is in his or her sinful heart. This treacherous deception can take any of us out of the race if we're not careful.

I recently read a *Wall Street Journal* article written by a well-known scholar on Islam and an even better known evolutionist. The Islamic scholar talked about a god who is unknowable and unapproachable. The evolutionist wrote that, given the complexity of evolution, God was irrelevant and superfluous. Neither expressed the slightest interest in following and obeying the God of the Bible. More troubling, the Web page containing the article had a section where readers could add their comments. I skimmed through the comments and quickly found that many of the contributors had at one time attended Bible-believing churches. They now chose not to believe in God because they couldn't imagine why a just and good God could allow so much suffering in the world. One person summed it up well: "I can't believe in a God who allows a six year-old girl to die of brain cancer." These people were quite bitter with Him, someone they insisted they did not believe in, because of something that had happened to them or others close to them. Rather than make every effort (2 Timothy 2:15, 2 Peter 1:5) to draw nearer to God and find out why He might have brought them or their loved one through such a trial, they chose to nurture their anger and bitterness against Him and eventually deny His existence. In essence, by choosing to follow some other belief system borne out of their bitterness, they have taken themselves out of the race and forfeited their prize, disqualified through grumbling.

It's important to remember that this doesn't have to be a permanent sentence. Solomon got sidetracked and forfeited the victor's crown when he chased after the false gods of his wives. Had he changed his mind and come back to God, he would have been back in the race and eligible for the prize. Solomon's father, warrior King David, the man after God's own heart, won the victor's crown even after committing adultery and murder. He repented of his sin, went back to God and followed Him the rest of his life.

The lure of the world is strong while we are on this earth living in our flesh and exposed to Satan's schemes. Pride, bitterness, greed, envy, and lust are powerful emotions. They can take each of us out of the race. Paul sounded the alarm to the rest of us in 1 Corinthians 10:12, when he said, "So, if you think you are standing firm, be careful that you don't fall!" He issued a similar warning in Colossians 2:18:

> Do not let anyone who delights in false humility and the worship of angels disqualify you for the prize. Such a person goes into great detail about what he has seen, and his unspiritual mind puffs him up with idle notions.

The word "disqualify" in this verse literally means "robbed," "cheated," or "seduced" out of the prize. Not salvation, mind you, but the reward for a life of service that has honored the true and living God. Similarly, John warns his readers in 2 John 1:8:

> *Watch out that you do not lose what you have worked for, but that you may be rewarded fully.*

May we heed these warnings and stay on the course, following Jesus Christ and not the lusts of our flesh. May we endure to win the prize.

A RACE AGAINST TIME AND DANGER

I want to close our discussion of the "Christian-as-runner" perspective with a story about a different kind of race. Instead of an athletic competition, this was a race against time and real, mortal danger. Given all we've talked about here in terms of preparation, endurance, and following the rules, I can't think of a more vivid way to describe how serious we need to be about running the race that is set before us.

Several years ago, I deployed aboard an aircraft carrier with a Navy jet fighter squadron. Before we were allowed to get underway, everyone aboard had to take a class in shipboard firefighting. I showed up at the big naval base in San Diego one Saturday morning to take the course. Several of the sailors were wondering why we had to learn shipboard firefighting techniques. "I'm a maintenance records clerk," "I'm an aviation electronics specialist," I heard them say. "Why do I need to be in this class?"

The instructors started the class by showing a short, grainy black-and-white film taken from the flight deck cameras aboard the *U.S.S. Forrestal* in the summer of 1967. At the time, this aircraft carrier was conducting combat operations off the coast of North Vietnam. The first few seconds of the film showed normal carrier flight operations. We could see the aircraft taxiing forward and positioning for launch and the flight deck crews scurrying about on the deck crowded with many aircraft. Suddenly the camera swung rapidly toward the aft end of the ship, where a thin smoke trail stuck out, like a pencil, from the wing of one aircraft directly into the fuselage of another jet.

The stricken aircraft, loaded with bombs, was now on fire. We watched as the primary damage control party moved toward the black smoke and the spreading fire, which had quickly engulfed several nearby aircraft, each loaded with multiple one-thousand pound bombs. Things were rapidly escalating out of control and time was critical. A couple of the damage control specialists ran up to the burning aircraft and the red-hot bombs, trying to put out the fire with their hand-held fire extinguishers. The rest of the damage control crew worked furiously to get fire hoses extended toward the flames.

What happened next sent a visible shudder through our classroom full of sailors and instantly removed any sense of doubt as to why we were there.

The movie screen literally turned white with the explosions of the first bombs that cooked off under the intense heat of the burning jet fuel. The horrific inferno obliterated several aircraft and wiped out the primary damage control party. We absorbed the unbelievable death and destruction captured on film in the blink of an eye. We sat transfixed by the ferocity of the exploding bombs, the showering flames of burning fuel and metal, the sailors running from the fire and as quickly turning around and running back into it to try to save their badly wounded shipmates. The secondary damage control party rushed in to fight the fires. Just as suddenly, they were annihilated by more exploding bombs.

The crew of the *Forrestal* was in a desperate race against the spreading fire to save the ship. Most of the remaining sailors aboard the ship had no prior training on how to fight a shipboard fire, and this was the worst possible moment to learn. Over the next twenty-four hours, the crew managed to extinguish the fires and keep the ship afloat. But it came at a terrible cost. Over 160 sailors were killed and an equal number badly wounded. The ship was out of commission for almost nine months. Worse yet, according to the investigation that was conducted afterward, many of the deaths and much of the damage need not have happened.

Because the ship's firefighting expertise was contained in the two damage control teams that were killed in the early moments of this inferno, the untrained crew used conflicting and counterproductive methods to put out the fire.

One group would lay down fire-quenching foam and another would spray water on the foam, washing it away and nullifying its effect. Other teams sprayed water into the bomb holes in the flight deck, spreading fuel, causing electrical short-circuits—and more fires—and destroying sensitive electrical and electronic components in the decks below. Their efforts, carried out with the best of intentions, actually put the ship in greater peril.

The investigating commission recommended that everyone deploying aboard Navy ships would learn how to fight shipboard fires. In the forty-plus years since the *Forrestal* fire, several Navy ships have been damaged by enemy action. These ships and the lives of many sailors have been saved because every crewmember now has the appropriate training and correctly-focused confidence to defeat a deadly fire when it occurs. When our class of sailors sailed from San Diego aboard the aircraft carrier *U.S.S. Nimitz*, we were confident in our ability to contain a shipboard fire, help save our ship and rescue our shipmates.

I wish there were a Christian movie that could generate the same effect on the twenty-first-century church as the *Forrestal* fire movie did on our room full of sailors. Everyone in our classroom that day became a diehard, born-again believer in knowing how to fight shipboard fires. We became serious and focused, and made every effort to learn what was being taught.

We knew we'd need moral courage, knowledge, self-control, and endurance to fight and defeat a raging, deadly fire.

How much more does God's training program, as Peter says in 2 Peter 1:3–4, equip us Christians for "life and godliness" so that we can perform in the time of mortal and eternal danger? Think about the pastor who is ministering to the adult movie industry. If he's not well-trained and equipped with moral courage, knowledge, self-control, endurance, and the reflection of God's character—and if he's not backed up by people who are—he will get swallowed by the raging fires of Satan. He will be like the primary damage control party, taken out in the earliest moments and leaving behind those who, lacking proper training, use counterproductive methods to fight the flames.

With this in mind, God wants each of us to be able to charge into a world raging with sin and help rescue those perishing from the cruel, deadly lies of our vicious enemy. He wants you and me to move away from "Christian couch-potato-hood," and to train, ahead of time, to respond effectively as a useful instrument of His work.

In 2 Peter 1:5, Peter tells us, "*for this very reason* [italics mine], make every effort to add to your faith" the attributes that bring about godliness. He encourages us in verse 8, "For if you possess these qualities in increasing measure, they will keep you from being ineffective and unproductive in your knowledge of our Lord Jesus Christ." This is what the "Christian-as-runner" perspective is all about: training with purpose, supplying and building up the qualities of the champion in increasing measure, becoming stronger and more mature to be partakers in the divine nature of His holiness. God wants us to be able to run according to the rules and win the victor's crown. As 2 Peter 1:10–11 says:

> *Therefore, my brothers, be all the more eager to make your calling and election sure. For if you do these things, you will never fall,*
>
> *And you will receive a rich welcome into the eternal kingdom of our Lord and Savior Jesus Christ.*

THE FARMER

Paul, in 2 Timothy 3:6, points to our third perspective for the Christian who is seeking God's will. Here, he says, "The hardworking farmer should be the first to eat from his own crops."

Farming is mentioned often in the Bible, most likely because it's what most people did when it was written. Many deep principles of wisdom are found in this way of life. In this verse, Paul hints at another of God's promises: our life is not supposed to be all sacrifice and suffering here on earth while we patiently wait for the rewards and joys of the next life. There are rewards to be realized and blessings to be enjoyed here and now.

Let's go to the very beginning. Farming starts with Adam.

ADAM'S FIRST JOB

In Genesis 2, God created Adam and gave him a job before He gave him a wife. Verse 15 tells us God "assigned" Adam to work the Garden of Eden. The popular English versions of the Bible say that he was told to "cultivate and keep it," "work it and take care of it," or "dress it and keep it."

We tend to think Adam and Eve were out there frolicking through the Garden in their birthday suits, chasing butterflies and soaking up the sunshine, enjoying their idyllic existence before they took that fateful bite of fruit. There are hints, though, that Adam, in his perfect and sinless state and created in the image of God, was much smarter than any man who has ever lived. It is more likely that tending the Garden of Eden was a complex operation, much different from anything we know today. Adam was able to effectively manage it as God's foreman or steward. Apparently, managing the Garden didn't seem like "work" as we understand the word today. Adam lived in a state of innocence and close fellowship with God, and his activities were unencumbered by the kind of natural resistance we know too well today.

It was after he and Eve sinned that God put a curse on Adam and permanently changed his work environment. In Genesis 3:17–19, God told Adam:

> *Cursed is the ground because of you; through painful toil you will eat of it all the days of your life. It will produce thorns and thistles for you, and you will eat the plants of the field.*

> *By the sweat of your brow you will eat your food until you return to the ground, since from it you were taken; for dust you are and to dust you will return.*

God booted Adam and Eve out of the Garden and gave him a new job. He had to work the ground and grow the food that would sustain him and his family. The ground, now cursed, from then on would bring forth things Adam couldn't eat. He had to sweat to grow the food he and his family could eat, and "work" became the four-letter word you and I so often detest today. Any farmer will tell you, after a hard day's labor, that he or she deeply understands this part of Adam's curse. At the same time, it was part of God's overall plan to redeem Adam and his descendents. The word "seed" came up more than once when God pronounced the curses on Adam and Eve, his work, and the way she would bring children into the world. He used the word in a promise of a Savior. In Genesis 3:15, God told Eve that one of her distant-future children was the "seed" that would bring redemption to the world.

GOD'S PRINCIPLE: SEEDS IN OUR HANDS

Many people, in their search for God's will, get hung up on what they need to do for themselves and what they must leave to Him. The principles of farming shed some light on this problem. Take a look at Isaiah 55:8–11:

> *"For my thoughts are not your thoughts, neither are your ways my ways," declares the Lord.*

> *"As the heavens are higher than the earth, so are my ways higher than your ways and my thoughts than your thoughts.*

> *"As the rain and the snow come down from heaven, and do not return to it without watering the earth and making it bud and flourish, so that it yields seed for the sower and bread for the eater,*

> *"So is my word that goes out from my mouth: It will not return to me empty, but will accomplish what I desire and achieve the purpose for which I sent it."*

In His creation, God set up a self-contained ecological system composed of earth, atmosphere, sunshine, and organic material. It enables another system, the social-economic one in which we live, sleep, work, and eat. This system of human interaction is also the one through which He has chosen to fulfill His eternal purposes for mankind's redemption. Using a significant word we'll look at again, it is the "economy" of His ultimate plan. We often don't know God's higher purposes, but we do know we have to eat, and we know we have to work to get our food.

Isaiah 28:23–29 gets even more specific:

> *Listen and hear my voice; pay attention and hear what I say. When a farmer plows for planting, does he plow continually? Does he keep on breaking up and harrowing the soil?*
>
> *When he has leveled the surface, does he not sow caraway and scatter cummin? Does he not plant wheat in its place, barley in its plot, and spelt in its field? His God instructs him and teaches him the right way.*
>
> *Caraway is not threshed with a sledge, nor is a cartwheel rolled over cummin; caraway is beaten out with a rod, and cummin with a stick.*
>
> *Grain must be ground to make bread; so one does not go on threshing it forever. Though he drives the wheels of his threshing cart over it, his horses do not grind it.*
>
> *All this also comes from the Lord Almighty, wonderful in counsel and magnificent in wisdom.*

These passages from Isaiah show how certain aspects of farming depend on God while others clearly depend on us. We can't make it rain or cause the earth to nourish the seeds. We can't make them bud and flourish to provide seed for the sower and bread for the eater. However, we can learn to divide, prepare, plant, and cultivate individual plots of land to grow different crops. We can learn the different methods to harvest and process various types of grain. The grain isn't going to grind itself to make bread, nor will the horses do it. We've got to do this work ourselves. Matthew Henry, the great nineteenth-century Bible commentator, made an interesting observation of Isaiah 28:27–28. If God hadn't revealed the principles of farming to certain people who'd eventually become good at it, he said, we'd be trying to farm the sand on the beach and would eventually starve to death.

Now, some might read Isaiah 28:26 and think we can wait for God to show us how to earn our keep. Can you imagine a person setting out to be a farmer, buying a field, and waiting for God to parachute down the "farming instruction manual" or show up personally to instruct him? Think back to the crazy, mystical ways people try to discern God's will and this doesn't sound so far-fetched. No, God enables the farmer to learn, but he or she must learn from other farmers or experiment with new methods. This is the same principle that holds in most any other field. You want to be an engineer? You study engineering. You want to be an accountant? You learn the principles of accounting. You want to drive a forklift? You've got to learn to operate it!

Our problem is this: *I want to be an engineer, accountant, or forklift operator, but does God want me to be that? What's God's role in this decision?* Zechariah 10:1 says, "Ask the Lord for rain in the springtime; it is the Lord who makes the storm clouds. He gives showers of rain to men, and plants of the field to everyone." In Matthew 5:45, Jesus said of His Father, "He causes his sun to rise on the evil and the good, and sends rain on the righteous and the unrighteous."

We can extend this to today's world: God provides the overall economy in which you and I find work. More specifically, He provides the circumstances in which you and I can do a certain job. The job will be one that:

1. Appeals to us,

2. We're good at,

3. We must learn to do out of necessity.

He decides which of these circumstances applies to us at a given time. I don't know about you, but I've experienced all three at different times of my life. I have been fortunate enough to have appealing jobs that played to my strengths. Many times, I had to take a job I disliked because it was the only one available. This was not by accident. God narrowed my choices and led me to that job. He used it for His higher purposes to teach me something or use me to meet another person's need. Here is our true choice: we can either submit to His plan or we can rebel and go our own way. God uses these circumstances to test the intent of our heart and for preparing us to execute the missions He's chosen for us in the context of this "economy."

In addition, God has created the "seasons" of corporate growth and decline, what the business world calls market lifecycles. The individual decisions of millions of people, buying and selling, manufacturing and transforming, make up the overall economy that some people use for good and others for evil. Adam Smith, in his landmark book on economics, *The Wealth of Nations*, called the market forces that create an economy the "invisible hand." The Bible, in Proverbs 16:11, attributes these market forces to God Himself: "Honest scales and balances are from the Lord; all the weights in the bag are of his making."

Paul, in 1 Corinthians 15:37–38, gave a short tutorial on farming to provide more insights for the Christian-as-farmer:

> *When you sow, you do not plant the body that will be, but just a seed, perhaps of wheat or of something else.*

> *But God gives it a body as he has determined, and to each kind of seed he gives its own body.*

God has programmed what will come from the seed He gives us to start our work. We don't know what it will look like when it's fully mature. Similarly, James 5:7 encourages us:

> *Be patient, then, brothers, until the Lord's coming. See how the farmer waits for the land to yield its valuable crop and how patient he is for the autumn and spring rains.*

These verses point to a fundamental truth: to successfully farm a field, we have to follow particular guidelines. It takes soil, seeds, sunshine and rain, as well as time and patience to grow a crop for food. The word "patience" used here in James 5:7 literally means "to wait," to anticipate a delay and have forbearance until it happens. It is different from the word we saw in James 1:3 and Hebrews 12:1, which meant "endurance." In few walks of life does God give us a fully mature, fruit-bearing plant. We instead get a set of ingredients that require us to add work. Our work includes fertilizing, planting, cultivating, tilling, pruning, cutting, threshing, and waiting: the same activities a farmer must put into the field to bring about an abundant harvest. Rather than get discouraged when the plants don't pop through the ground on a particular day, does the farmer give up and plant something else? No, he or she continues to work and wait, knowing a broader set of rules is involved. The farmer does what is necessary to make the plants as healthy and viable as possible so they will bear much fruit at the harvest—which he or she knows is coming.

IF GOD HAD WANTED MAN TO FLY …

I read a book that said the British ended up ruling the world because their soil was bad. According to this book, they had to work hard to coax any food out of the harsh and rocky British Isles so they could eat. This difficult effort strengthened them to become survivors and risk takers, and in turn, made them more willing to build sailing ships, explore beyond their own territories, and conquer new lands. In the process, they built a global empire that lasted almost four hundred years. The Spanish did much the same thing, and the Dutch conquered the North Sea by constructing huge dikes and polders to reclaim and farm land below sea level.

How does this apply to you and me in trying to find God's will? There was a time when people said, "If God wanted man to fly, He would have given us wings." Well, God didn't give us wings, but He gave us something else. He gave us Bernoulli's Principle, which is based on one of Isaac Newton's fundamental laws of motion called "the conservation of energy." Daniel Bernoulli, living in Switzerland in 1738, published a book called *Hydrodynamique* containing a set of mathematical formulas that describes how fluids flow under pressure. Others used these mathematical formulas to design "airfoils" or wings that could generate "lift" based on how they were shaped. This explains how birds, airplanes, and even helicopters are able to fly. God's plan was not to give us wings. Instead, he gave us a set of physical laws and principles—and the wisdom, desire, and fortitude to figure out how to apply them—and let us design and build machines that can fly. This is quite a miracle, and is one I have appreciated while flying military helicopters and racking up frequent flyer miles on several major airlines.

We may hear someone tell a story of how God momentarily suspended the laws of physics to work a miracle. Even if the story is true, it's clear that He expects you and me to live in accordance with those physical laws as we go about our business each day. "What goes up must come down." "The higher you go, the harder you fall." "It's not the fall that hurts; it's the sudden stop at the end." And so on. These sayings are passed down from parents to children, teachers to students, and experts to amateurs, to explain the laws of physics.

None of us, being of sound mind, will take a walk out of a ten-story window. We know what happens next. On the other hand, history is full of examples of scientists, engineers, inventors, and tinkerers who have found ways to make our lives more convenient and productive by creatively managing and applying the laws of physics. The airplane is a prime example. Before the Wright brothers got their mechanical contraption into the air at Kitty Hawk in December 1903, powered flight was a dream. These two bicycle makers from Dayton, Ohio, strapped an internal combustion engine to a set of wooden and cloth wings that followed Bernoulli's Principle and got the Wright Flyer going fast enough to generate lift. The dream became reality.

Today, the biggest challenge about getting on an airliner and flying halfway around the world is going through the security line and paying extra for baggage. One of my business colleagues works for a start-up company with manufacturing facilities in China. He makes the trip from Atlanta to Beijing or Shanghai twice a month and there's no longer any sense of wonder or excitement in it for him. A hundred years ago, a trip to and from China within a week would have been considered an absolute miracle. Now, it's just hard work, a long and exhausting commute through a whole slew of time zones.

Proverbs 28:19 says, "He who works his land will have abundant food, but the one who chases fantasies will have his fill of poverty." I can almost hear the voices of those from ages past who used this verse to warn us against trying to build an airplane, a car, a bridge, or a cell phone. Think about it this way: In the book of Genesis, God told Adam and Noah to subdue, cultivate, and replenish the earth. He gave them the raw materials to do so and the brains to figure out how. He never told them what is possible or what is a fantasy. He told them to get out there and figure it out for themselves. In the twenty-first century, when we've already put a human on the moon and enjoy instantaneous, global communications, what is the "land" we are to subdue, cultivate and replenish, and what is truly a fantasy?

Until about two hundred years ago, most people worked on farms, trying to grow food. It took the majority of people in a society working their little patch of land to produce enough to feed themselves and their animals. A boy would expect to take on the same work as his father, be it as a farmer, a fisherman, a blacksmith, or a shoemaker. The boy, on average, could expect to travel no more than fifty miles from his birthplace during his entire lifetime. A young girl's prospects were even more limited. She would likely grow up and marry someone known to her family, and be expected to give birth to many sons who would continue working the family farm or trade.

During the past two hundred years, the technological advances of the Industrial and Information Ages have enabled most people in the Western world, and more recently in India and China, to leave the farms and go to work in factories or office buildings. Today, fewer than two percent of Americans work in agriculture and they feed the rest of us better than at any time in history. Recent technological advances in manufacturing, as well as offshore competition from India and China, are now causing more and more people to leave the factories for service- or information-oriented jobs.

Why do I bring this up? In the days before these huge leaps in technology, far fewer jobs were available for someone to choose to do during his or her life. People rarely changed careers. Today, the Dictionary of Occupational Titles published by the U.S. Department of Labor lists literally thousands of jobs. The average American can expect to change careers several times in his or her lifetime. As you and I seek God's will, we have more choices available to us than ever before in history. It's now much easier to move halfway around the world and begin a new life, start a business, connect with a global community, get access to information, and make the decision to do something different.

It's gotten crazier in the past fifteen years with the rise of the World Wide Web and our globally connected, real-time world. Thomas Friedman of the *New York Times* wrote an interesting book several years ago called *The World Is Flat*, describing how the Internet and global communications are leveling the playing field around the world and opening up opportunities—and threats— from many different places.

A few years ago, I managed a team of software engineers who were working in Bangalore, India. I never went there or met the team face to face. Instead, I was on the phone, email, or Web conferences with them every day from my office outside San Francisco. Using the power of the Internet, our team was able to build, release, and support a global business software application in less than four months. Several times in the past decade, I've managed global teams of software engineers, marketing analysts and military personnel, using fre-quent conference calls or Web-based collaboration sessions to communicate with people all over the world.

Several recent books have been written about how these technological changes are going to affect Christians and the church. It's quite possible that, ten years from now, some of the biggest churches on earth will be "virtual," existing not in a geographical location but on social networking websites such as Facebook or Twitter. We may congregate together over our iPhones and Blackberries, having "church" anywhere and almost continuously rather than in a certain building at ten o'clock on Sunday morning.

I can almost see the red faces of some pastors, their blood pressure rising as they read this. Sorry, pastors, but this is a tide of history, much like the invention of the printing press in the mid-1400s that brought about the Protestant Reformation. Emerging technology will have a huge effect on how ordinary Christians seek God's will and follow Him day to day from outside the walls of a physical church auditorium. Some churches have sold their buildings and are using the money from the sale and their now much-reduced operating costs to fund more missions work. As author Dan Poynter said:

You can't change the wind, but you can trim your sails.

In the midst of all these changes, we can easily lose sight of the big picture of how things truly work in God's spiritual and physical realms. How do we know what God wants from us in such chaotic times? We have to remind ourselves that nothing in this crazy world has taken Him by surprise. The Bible has laid down clear and timeless principles we should be aware of as we make our choices, big and little, and carry them out.

One principle a farmer knows intimately well, for example, is to understand the times and seasons for planting, cultivating, harvesting, and letting the land rest. Knowing we are on the threshold of such major societal changes being influenced by new technology, now is the time for Christians to be planting and cultivating—and preparing for rain.

PREPARING FOR RAIN: WORKING AND WAITING

Because we live in such an "instant" twenty-first century world, we tend to forget many of the timeless lessons about life our ancestors understood from farming the soil. We forget, as Ecclesiastes 3 tells us, there is a time and a season for everything. We forget, in our service-based economy, we occasionally have to move a big rock out of the way to plant our seeds or get the water to flow the right way. Sometimes we must uproot and burn plants that are no longer productive. Joseph Schumpeter, a twentieth-century economist, came up with a widely-used term for this particular aspect of the economic lifecycle, calling it "creative destruction."

Too often, we forget we must cultivate, prepare, and do something in our field every day. I mentioned Sherwood Baptist Church of Albany, Georgia, and their recent movie *Facing the Giants.* My favorite scene in that movie is when Mr. Bridges, a godly older man, walks down a hallway in the high school, running one hand along the wall lockers, holding his Bible in the other, praying for the students and the school. The football coach, Grant Taylor, is going through a tough time with some of the school leaders and parents because the team hasn't been winning games. Coach Taylor believes he's about to be fired from his job.

Mr. Bridges walks into the coach's office and tells him that he feels led of God to encourage him that the Lord is not yet finished with him at this school. He goes on to tell Coach Taylor a story about two farmers who were praying to God, asking Him to bring rain to water their fields. One, he says, prepared his fields for the rain; the other didn't. He asks, "Which one was trusting God?" Grant Taylor says, "The one who prepared his fields." Mr. Bridges nods and responds, "Coach, God will send the rain when He's ready. You need to prepare your field to receive it."

What a great picture of God's will for the rest of us! God will do His part, but He expects us to do our part. Our part is to prepare our fields to receive His rain! As we look into our own lives, how do we do our part? Take a look at Ecclesiastes 11:4:

Whoever watches the wind will not plant; whoever looks at the clouds will not reap.

This verse is commonly interpreted to mean that we can always come up with a reason to not work. "If it's windy, the seeds will blow away before I plant them! If it's raining, I won't be able to harvest the crops! Better stay inside until tomorrow!" Ecclesiastes 11:6 continues:

Sow your seed in the morning, and at evening let not your hands be idle, for you do not know which will succeed, whether this or that, or whether both will do equally well.

God chooses not to tell the farmer ahead of time how much He will bless his labor. He does, however, tell the farmer to work hard. Proverbs 24:30–34 is an instructive passage, one I often think about when I feel like sleeping in while there's work to be done (which happens more than I'd like to admit):

I walked by the field of a lazy person, the vineyard of one lacking sense. I saw that it was overgrown with thorns. It was covered with weeds, and its walls were broken down.

Then, as I looked and thought about it, I learned this lesson: A little extra sleep, a little more slumber, a little folding of the hands to rest—and poverty will pounce on you like a bandit; scarcity will attack you like an armed robber.

This is a great story to tell people when they say, "Well, God is in control, so I'll wait on Him to lead me." What are we waiting for? God has already told us what to do. Proverbs 20:4 is even more direct, "If you are too lazy to plow in the right season, you will have no food at the harvest." God is telling us to get out there in the fields and prepare them for rain.

Instead of a patch of land, our field today is more likely a job in a large company, a small business, or a government agency. It can be a school, a neighborhood or the home. As Henry Blackaby said in *Experiencing God*, it is the place where you and I are right now, and God is already at work there. It's up to us to join Him in that work. He's given us seeds to plant and cultivate, turning into fruit that we are to harvest. This fruit is the reward of our labors, not only in the effect we have on the lives of those around us but also on the work itself. God expects us to do a good job and deliver results wherever we find ourselves.

The seasons or lifecycles in these fields may be more subtle, less predictable, and longer in duration than farming's annual seasons. But they do follow a similar pattern and can be discerned to a large extent, if not predicted. For centuries, farmers have dug up ground and planted seeds, waiting for rain that may or may not come. God, for His purposes, may choose not to bring the rain, but this doesn't release the farmer from the duty of getting out in the field, working it and preparing for the rain when it does come. If the fields are ready and the rain comes, He promises a bountiful harvest. Isaiah 30:23 says, "He will also send you rain for the seed you sow in the ground, and the food that comes from the land will be rich and plentiful. In that day your cattle will graze in broad meadows."

In the business world, I worked on several corporate projects where our senior executives hired high-powered management consultants to advise them on their marketing strategies and business plans. The management consultants, some of whom were making over half a million dollars a year, came in with elaborate PowerPoint presentations and Excel spreadsheets, for which they charged us hundreds of thousands, if not millions of dollars. I noticed how, almost every time, they showed the same "planting," "cultivation," "harvest," and "decline" lifecycle familiar to any farmer. Whether you realize it or not, shrewd financial investors and venture capitalists also track the companies in their portfolio according to the same pattern—and make millions for their insights.

On a more personal level, I remember a time several years ago when a good friend of mine was looking for a job. One prospective employer had asked him to submit a résumé, so my friend called and asked me to come over and help him put one together. While we were sitting at his kitchen table working on the résumé, his wife came in and said, "Why are you doing that? If God wants him to get the job, he'll get it." I believe her reasoning could be translated like this: "If God wants you to eat, He'll send down a meal on a platter three times a day."

Has He done that for you lately? No? Me neither.

In His judgment of Adam, which we all share, God chose to make us work for our food. Instead of a buffet table with a full meal, he's given us the basic elements to generate food: seed, seasons, soil, and rain, along with clear instructions to go out into the field and get to work. If we don't, we might be able to find enough seeds that have randomly fallen in our field to produce a little bit of food, but there will certainly not be enough to feed us or our families for very long. In the New Testament, Paul told a group of church members something similar in 2 Thessalonians 3:6–12:

> In the name of the Lord Jesus Christ, we command you, brothers, to keep away from every brother who is idle and does not live according to the teaching you received from us.
>
> For you yourselves know how you ought to follow our example. We were not idle when we were with you, nor did we eat anyone's food without paying for it. On the contrary, we worked night and day, laboring and toiling so that we would not be a burden to any of you.
>
> We did this, not because we do not have the right to such help, but in order to make ourselves a model for you to follow.
>
> For even when we were with you, we gave you this rule: "If a man will not work, he shall not eat."

We hear that some among you are idle. They are not busy; they are busybodies. Such people we command and urge in the Lord Jesus Christ to settle down and earn the bread they eat.

The word "idle" used throughout this passage is the Greek word *ataktohs*, which the KJV translates as "walking disorderly." The NASB uses the phrase "leading an undisciplined life." Paul cautioned these Christians to be diligent, to settle down and get to work to earn their bread, and warned against an unruly, idle, undisciplined life that leads to waste and meddling in the affairs of others. Paul was so serious about this that he twice invoked the name of the Lord Jesus Christ as he wrote down this instruction.

Given these strict warnings from God's Word, why do so many of us think it's a good strategy to wait for Him to bring the rain and a miraculous harvest without working to prepare our fields? Surely all of us have heard stories of people hitting the jackpot or literally tripping over a major opportunity that has plopped down on the path in front of them. Sometimes God does move in ways that circumvent our plans and best efforts. And, yes, there are encouragements in the Bible to wait on the Lord. We need to remind ourselves that the word used for "wait" in those verses always means to endure. It's not the same word James used to describe waiting for the harvest. In this case, it means to work the field through the planting and cultivation phases and then, at the appointed time, to bring in the harvest. I've seen too many Christians get sidetracked onto the path of least resistance, foregoing opportunities God has placed in front of them, because they were supposedly exercising "faith" by sitting there and doing nothing while waiting for Him to make the first move. Here is a key point: when He has given us such clear instructions to get to work, why are we waiting for anything else?

You might ask, "Where should I work? What if I can't find a job?"

Think of Joseph in the book of Genesis. He was sold into slavery by his brothers and eventually ended up in an Egyptian jail. He had little control over these circumstances, and at this point his options for employment were severely limited. The Bible says that Joseph worked hard and applied himself to the only job available—prison inmate—so much so that the jailer ended up letting him run the prison.

One day, God decided Joseph had had enough preparation to carry out an important mission in His ultimate plan. He miraculously placed him into an entirely different line of work as the Prime Minister of Egypt, second only to Pharaoh himself. Joseph did his part during the planting and cultivating seasons, working hard every day within the circumstances he was given. God did his part by bringing the rain at the right time, rewarding Joseph with an incredible mission—and opportunity. Remember that Joseph didn't stop trying to get out of jail. A couple of conversations with a butler and a baker come to mind. Like Paul in Acts 16, he made plans, but God opened and closed the doors. Like the blessed truth of Proverb 16:9, he may have planned his course, but the Lord determined his steps. More importantly, during his time in prison, Joseph learned to walk with God, to trust His guidance and endure the seasons He had set before him. Years later, God gave Joseph an even more abundant and fruitful harvest when he brought his family to Egypt and fulfilled a significant part of the Lord's ultimate plan for the nation of Israel. In the words of 2 Timothy 2:5, he was the first to enjoy the crops of his harvest.

How many Christians do only the minimum required to draw their paycheck at work? I've had pastors tell me, "Tom, just work for the weekend!" To the contrary, God expects us to fully apply ourselves in our work, wherever it is. Proverbs 22:29 says, "Do you see a man skilled in his work? He will serve before kings; he will not serve before obscure men." The word for "skilled" here is translated "diligent" in the KJV and "truly competent" in the NLT. One of the timeless principles of farming is that you can't take shortcuts to a bountiful harvest. The same thing is true in our world of work.

Proverbs 27:23–27 gives more insight into the skill and effort God expects of us:

> Be sure you know the condition of your flocks, give careful attention to your herds; for riches do not endure forever, and a crown is not secure for all generations.

> When the hay is removed and new growth appears and the grass from the hills is gathered in, the lambs will provide you with clothing, and the goats with the price of a field.

> You will have plenty of goats' milk to feed you and your family and to nourish your servant girls.

For a business person, here is a key passage from God's Word. It describes someone who works hard to stay on top of what's taking place throughout his or her entire, diversified business enterprise. This person is not working for the weekend or lying down and saying, "Well, if God wants me to have food and clothing, He'll provide." No, this person is actively working as a good steward of a range of different investments. He (or she) is wisely using every asset to provide for himself, his family, and his employees regardless of the season or market lifecycle.

Something similar to the "build an airplane instead of wish for wings" principle is at work here: when the crops are harvested, and while the farmer has to wait a year for the next crop to grow, he has raised lambs and goats that will provide food, clothing, and money for more investments. Today, a wise person tries to maintain a diversified portfolio and pays attention to it: the principles of market lifecycles and diversification can help us to effectively manage the talents, assets and circumstances God has given us. They apply to our households as well. Ecclesiastes 11:2 says, "Give portions to seven, yes to eight, for you do not know what disaster may come upon the land." What Solomon is saying here is, "Don't put all your eggs in one basket."

You may say, "Tom, I don't have the smarts to track a bunch of financial investments. Is that really what God wants from me?" Well, he may not want you or me to become a Wall Street wizard, but He does expect us to be good stewards of what He's given us. Keeping in mind, as Paul said 1 Corinthians 15:37–38, that God gives us seeds and not harvest-ready fruit, we know we've got to go out into the field and do the work that enables the harvest. So let's look at the best way we can educate and prepare ourselves to be effective workers in the fields where God has placed us.

STANDING ON THE SHOULDERS
OF GIANTS

Earlier, we looked at Isaiah 28, which describes specific ways a farmer dealt with different crops in those days. Verse 26 tells us, "His God instructs him and teaches him the right way."

I have to go back to this one again: do you wonder how that actually happened? Imagine God coming down to sit with each farmer and say, "Okay, pal, look here. Plant these seeds in this spot, dig those trenches over there, run the water that way. Oh, and make sure you change the oil in the John Deere tractor every three months." No, we can be sure the average farmer did not get this special treatment.

God did give Moses some specific instructions about land use and ownership, community sanitation and strict observance of seasonal feasts within the Law to thank the Lord for the fruits of the annual harvests. On the other hand, the specific lessons of how to farm the land were handed down from generation to generation in the form of spoken "tribal knowledge" or written instructions passed from father to son, master to apprentice, owner to tenant. God gave them the tools and the curiosity to experiment and innovate rather than provide a complete, specific set of instructions to follow. You and I learn in the same way to work in our own particular twenty-first-century field.

I'm sure those ancient Hebrew farmers asked the same questions you and I ask today: "How do I know what to do first? What's most important? If there are no shortcuts, do I have to learn everything from scratch? How do I do this the right way, according to your will?" God answers by giving us insights and opportunities, along with the sunshine and the rain—and the collected body of knowledge captured by those who've gone before us. We add the work effort, not only to execute, but to learn, manage and build up the body of knowledge.

Eugene Cernan, the commander of the Apollo 17 space mission, was the last human to leave a footprint on the moon. When he returned to earth on December 16, 1972, he quoted the famous seventeenth-century physicist Isaac Newton:

If I have seen further, it is by standing on the shoulders of giants.

Newton's laws of motion are what every engineer and scientist in the Apollo moon program had to learn and master in order to successfully build, test, launch, and recover the spacecraft—and their crews of astronauts—as they traveled to the moon and back. The engineers of the 1950s and 1960s were able to "stand on the shoulders of giants" to see their way to the moon, using past discoveries in math and science to accomplish what is undoubtedly the landmark engineering achievement of human history.

If you spend any time with someone who is a master in their field, you find they likely have a selection of authoritative references to which they repeatedly look for guidance—the works of the "giants" upon whose shoulders they stand. Most top military leaders read Sun Tzu's *The Art of War,* Karl von Clausewitz's *On War,* or Miyamoto Musashi's *A Book of Five Rings* on a regular basis, over and over again. Effective business managers regularly study leadership or strategy books. Almost every senior vice-president with whom I worked in the software business had a copy of Harvard Business School professor Michael Porter's classic *Competitive Strategy* on his or her desk—right next to Sun Tzu's *The Art of War!*

Before the invention of the printing press, before people could write down and widely distribute the collected body of knowledge for their field of work, a person would work for years as an apprentice to a master, learning the tricks of the trade before going on to practice that craft and pass on his own knowledge to the next generation. There's something to this. To become a champion in our field, only one shortcut works. We have to learn and understand the collected wisdom of the experts, "standing on the shoulders of the giants" who have gone before us.

A champion studies other champions and learns from them, always looking for new ways to increase performance, with his or her eye on the prize. The problem is that most of us have a hard time taking advice from others, especially in areas where our passions or fears are involved. It seems we have to make the mistakes ourselves before we can finally learn the lesson. A mother will tell her five-year-old child to not put his hand on the stove, but it's usually only after the toddler scorches his hand that he makes it his own personal rule: *Don't put your hand on a hot stove!* It's almost like each of us has this computer program hardwired into our heads, "Yeah, it may have worked out that way for you, but I'm different. I can get away with it." Imagine the Apollo engineers and scientists saying, "I don't believe in the laws of physics or gravity. Let's try to build a spacecraft without a descent-stage rocket motor or a reentry parachute, and go to the moon and back."

Sure, try it and see what happens.

I'm reminded of the old '60s TV comedy *Green Acres*, where New York lawyer Oliver Wendell Douglas and his lovely wife Lisa moved to a farm in the middle of nowhere. One day another farmer came by to visit Oliver and asked him how he was irrigating his crops. Just about then, Eb, Oliver's hired hand, walked up with a garden hose and a hand sprinkler. Oliver was certainly not standing on the shoulders of giants, learning the lessons countless farmers had passed down over the centuries before him, so he had to learn them himself—the hard way. And we think this is funny!

In our own spiritual lives, how many of us know of others who've gone against God's principles and suffered the consequences, only to let Satan deceive us into thinking it won't happen to us? Why do we think we can get away with violating God's moral laws of the universe when we know we can't violate His physical laws? How can we avoid the mistakes of others, and at the same time learn to become victorious Christians? The answer is the one we've heard time and again: become a student of the Bible, the Word of God, study the writings of great Christians from the past, listen to the sermons of godly preachers and pay attention to the wise counsel of mature Christians.

So, how's that going for you?

In today's fast-paced world, it's easy for Christians to get caught up in a channel surfing, fast-food approach to learning God's Word. We may go to church one hour a week and attend a home Bible study for another hour. Perhaps we'll listen to a sermon on the radio during our drive home from work or even sit through a podcast on our computer. We might go so far as to buy a book or two on how to study the Bible. God gives us the tools, curiosity, and insight to build practical knowledge for farming or business and makes us add the work as our part of the deal. He does the same thing when it comes to knowing God's Word. The writer of Psalm 119, the longest chapter in the Bible, gave 176 different reasons why he studied, learned, and obeyed God's laws. Chuck Missler of *Koinonia House Ministries*, in almost every one of his Bible studies, invokes Acts 17:11 as a warning:

> *Now the Bereans were of more noble character than the Thessalonians, for they received the message with great eagerness and examined the Scriptures every day to see if what Paul said was true.*

Victorious Christians want to learn what God says about truth, human nature, the principles of life, and our relationship with Him. We can't sit back and take someone else's word for it when we are warned in almost every book of the New Testament that so many false teachers have infiltrated the church. We want to examine the Scriptures every day to see if what we're hearing and seeing is true. We want to dig deeper and get beyond the fast-food mentality so many Christians practice in learning the Bible. We want to rely on its power to discern, as Hebrews 4:12 tells us, the thoughts and intents of the heart. We Christians-as-farmers want to work at it.

Some relevant advice along these lines can be found in Paul's New Testament letter to Titus. Another of Paul's missionary protégés, Titus had been sent to oversee a group of new Christians on Crete, an island in the Mediterranean Sea south of Greece and a way station on the major trade routes of the Roman Empire. Paul was counseling Titus how to lead the growing groups of Christian believers to become stronger in their faith, and to overcome the many obstacles that stood between them and a rich harvest of spiritual maturity and victory. In Titus 2:1–8, he gave some pointed advice on how they should conduct themselves as Christians:

You must teach what is in accord with sound doctrine. Teach the older men to be temperate, worthy of respect, self-controlled, and sound in faith, in love and in endurance.

Likewise, teach the older women to be reverent in the way they live, not to be slanderers or addicted to much wine, but to teach what is good.

Then they can train the younger women to love their husbands and children, to be self-controlled and pure, to be busy at home, to be kind, and to be subject to their husbands, so that no one will malign the word of God.

Similarly, encourage the young men to be self-controlled.

In everything set them an example by doing what is good. In your teaching show integrity, seriousness and soundness of speech that cannot be condemned, so that those who oppose you may be ashamed because they have nothing bad to say about us.

Like Timothy, who was not too far away in Ephesus, Titus was battling a group of people who were introducing false doctrine and leading new believers astray for personal gain. In Titus 1:10–11, Paul told him, "There are many rebellious people, mere talkers and deceivers, especially those of the circumcision group. They must be silenced, because they are *ruining whole households* [italics mine] by teaching things they ought not to teach—and that for the sake of dishonest gain." Paul repeats this message once again: we must be clear-minded and self-controlled, becoming proficient enough at God's Word to not be carried off by some attractive but deceptive and destructive scheme of Satan. We must effectively plant and cultivate the truth of God's Word in the field of our own heart. God promises us a rich harvest if we do so.

In Hebrews 5:11–14, Paul gave another group of believers some strong advice. These were people whom he thought by now should be mature, victorious Christians rather than unlearned beginners:

We have much to say about this, but it is hard to explain because you are slow to learn.

In fact, though by this time you ought to be teachers, you need someone to teach you the elementary truths of God's word all over again. You need milk, not solid food!

Anyone who lives on milk, being still an infant, is not acquainted with the teaching about righteousness.

But solid food is for the mature, who by constant use have trained themselves to distinguish good from evil.

Look at verse 14: we've seen this word "trained" before. It is the same word for "gymnasium" Paul used when talking about training for godliness in 1 Timothy 4:7–8 and Hebrews 12:11. A farmer becomes proficient through formal or on-the-job training, by standing on the shoulders of giants and using the tools of the trade. He or she has developed expertise, wisdom, and discipline, and can distinguish the good from the bad in bringing about a bountiful harvest. The same principle applies to the Christian-as-farmer.

GOD'S EXPECTED RETURN ON INVESTMENT

In Matthew 25:14–30 and Luke 19:13–26, Jesus told the well-known parable of the master and the talents. Here, a master gave "talents," or sums of money, to three servants and asked each of them to invest the money for him while he was out of the country. In Luke's passage, when the master came back, one servant brought in a tenfold return and the second brought back five times the initial investment. The third servant hid the money in a napkin.

"Here," the third servant said to the master, "You can have it back."

The master was quite pleased with the first two servants' results and rewarded them for their investment. He was not at all happy, however, with the third. This servant told him, "I was afraid of you. I know you're a stern, exacting and harsh [the Greek word is *austeron*, from which we get "austere"] master, and that you harvest where you have not scattered seed." Rather insulting, wouldn't you think? The master said to him, "Hey, buddy, you could have at least put it in the bank so I'd earn some interest!" Then he punished the third servant and threw him out, giving his talent to the first servant.

Where I come from, the returns on investment Jesus mentioned in this story are some mind-boggling numbers. A Wall Street investment manager who makes twenty percent on his or her money is considered a "master of the universe." When I worked in the software business, my team would do an "ROI analysis" to determine the return on investment for a given project. If we convinced our senior vice presidents that the project could make more money than we'd get by keeping the project funds in the bank, earning interest, we'd get approval for it. We're talking single-digit percentages from the bank, so if we brought in a ten-percent return on investment, we had hit a home run.

So, what is Jesus saying here, talking about tenfold or one-thousand percent returns on investment? None of the commentaries I looked at while studying these passages would tackle that one. The Greek words *talentos* and *mina* translated as "talent," "money," or "pound" in these two passages refer to a specific weight of silver or gold used as money. Jesus gave no indication that he thought the first two servants had brought back spectacular returns. Rather, he seems to suggest these returns were characteristic of good and faithful stewardship, to be rewarded accordingly.

I wonder how the markets worked back in Jesus' day to bring in those kinds of returns which are way beyond what can be expected by your typical twenty-first-century corporate finance department. Take a look at what the third servant said in Matthew 25:24, "I knew you harvested where you did not plant, and gathered where you did not cultivate." The first two servants most likely used the money in their agriculturally-focused economy to buy land and seed they could plant, cultivate, and harvest. They could then sell the crops to earn this kind of return. In the same way, God gives us the basic ingredients we are to manage such that we bring in the huge and, according to Jesus Christ, expected returns on investment.

Jesus Christ told a similar parable in Matthew 13, Mark 4 and Luke 8. This is the familiar story of the sower and the seed. The sower planted the seed which resulted in four different outcomes, depending on the condition of the ground where he worked. The first seeds fell along a path and birds came and ate them up. The second bunch fell on stony ground where the seeds quickly grew in the shallow soil but just as quickly withered and died. The third group fell among thorns and was choked out before it could grow and bear fruit. The fourth set fell on good, fertile ground and grew to bring forth an abundant harvest with the familiar return on investment: thirty, sixty, a hundredfold.

What do these parables mean to the Christian-as-farmer?

It is God's desire that we bear a lot of fruit with the seeds He has given us. In John 15:8 (KJV), Jesus tells His disciples, "Herein is my Father glorified, that ye bear much fruit; so shall ye be my disciples." 2 Peter 1:8 (KJV), a verse we looked at in the previous section, says, "For if these things be in you, and abound, they make you that ye shall neither be barren nor unfruitful in the knowledge of our Lord Jesus Christ." What things? The things Peter listed in 2 Peter 1:5–7: Faith, moral courage, knowledge, self-control, endurance, godliness, brotherly kindness and love. In Galatians 5:22–23, Paul lists the *fruit* of the Spirit as "love, joy, peace, patience, kindness, goodness, faithfulness, gentleness and self-control." Note the similarities. These spiritual qualities are the fruit God expects us to bear and in the process gain a thousand-percent return on investment.

How will we know we're being successful at this? Is there a way we can measure the rate of return on the fruit we bear for God without trying to rack up a bunch of notches on our "soul-winner's stick" or taking a poll of our friends to see how spiritual they think we are?

I believe the Bible shows us how to go about this work. For the Christian, "these things" of 2 Peter 1 and the fruits of the Spirit of Galatians 5:22–23 enable us to be the farmers whom God will use to plant and cultivate the seeds of His grace in the hearts and lives of others. He then transforms these seeds into a harvest of fruit that can be accounted to us. We need to keep some specific things in mind. To start, look at John 15. Here, Jesus explained the "bearing fruit" concept to His disciples. Specifically, in verses 4 and 5, He says:

Remain in me, and I will remain in you. No branch can bear fruit by itself; it must remain in the vine. Neither can you bear fruit unless you remain in me.

I am the vine; you are the branches. If a man remains in me and I in him, he will bear much fruit; apart from me you can do nothing.

Jesus stresses this point about remaining (or abiding, as the KJV says), in Him. Unlike some people I know who used to keep score on how many "souls" they'd won to the Lord, we need to put our focus on responding to the needs around us and the mission opportunities God places in our way. Jesus said we are the branches of the vine, not the vine itself. Nor are we the gardener. That job is taken by God the Father, as Jesus said in John 15:1.

Think of it this way: God is the owner of a field, and has decided to hire you and me as laborers to bring in His harvest. Jesus used this same analogy in Matthew 9:37–38, Luke 10:2 and John 4:35. As laborers in the harvest, we are to do the jobs He assigns us in the field where He leads us to work. He has the overall plan and responsibility for bringing in the harvest. He's using us as the hired help to do the work and will pay us accordingly. Jesus touched on this principle in Mark 4:26–27:

> He also said, "This is what the kingdom of God is like. A man scatters seed on the ground. Night and day, whether he sleeps or gets up, the seed sprouts and grows, though he does not know how.

> "All by itself the soil produces grain—first the stalk, then the head, then the full kernel in the head. As soon as the grain is ripe, he puts the sickle to it, because the harvest has come."

Notice that God didn't plant the seed or put the sickle to the mature crop of grain. The man did those jobs while God grew the grain. Compare this to what Paul said in 1 Corinthians 3:6-10:

> I planted the seed, Apollos watered it, but God made it grow. So neither he who plants nor he who waters is anything, but only God, who makes things grow.

> The man who plants and the man who waters have one purpose, and each will be rewarded according to his own labor.

> For we are God's fellow workers; you are God's field.

It is critical for us to understand this division of labor in the "Christian-as-farmer" perspective. If we're submitted to Him and willing to do what He requires of us to bring in the crops, we can be sure we're aligned with His plan and growing the fruits of the Spirit in our hearts. He will not only show us the fruit of the harvest in His time, but will also make us known by our fruits.

KNOWN BY OUR FRUITS: GOOD WORKS

You've probably heard the saying, "By their fruits you will know them." It comes from the Sermon on the Mount in Matthew 7:15–16 (KJV), where Jesus warned His listeners:

> *"Beware of false prophets, which come to you in sheep's clothing, but inwardly they are ravening wolves.*

> *Ye shall know them by their fruits. Do men gather grapes of thorns, or figs of thistles?"*

"You shall know them by their fruits." What does this mean? I've met church people who call themselves "licensed fruit inspectors" as they go around critiquing the actions of others. This is probably not what Jesus had in mind. Instead, He joins virtually all of the New Testament writers in warning us about those people who come into the church and lead others astray for personal gain. This is a reality we must constantly guard against, not only from others, but also, as Beth Moore warned us, from letting the same thing happen in our own hearts.

God has given us the job to plant and water the seeds of the Word of God in the hearts of those with whom we come into contact every day, wherever we are. At the same time, according to Matthew 13:19, Mark 4:15, and Luke 8:12, Satan is trying to snatch the seeds away so these people will not come to Jesus Christ. Here's where the connection is made between our individual actions and a fruitful harvest. Paul, in Titus 3:14 (NASB), said, "Our people must also learn to engage in good deeds to meet pressing needs, so that they will not be unfruitful." Who are "our people?" You and me! Paul said almost the same thing in Colossians 1:10, "And we pray this in order that you may live a life worthy of the Lord and may please him in every way: *bearing fruit in every good work* [emphasis mine], growing in the knowledge of God."

What are these good works?

The phrase "good work" or "good works" appears twenty-eight times in the New Testament. "Good" is translated from two different Greek words used almost interchangeably. They mean essentially the same thing: "noble," "beneficial," or "praiseworthy." The word for "work" is *ergos,* from which we get "energy." This word has two meanings. The most familiar is "effort," in the form of individual actions or accomplishments. The second is a collection of activities that make up a complete enterprise, such as the terms "public works," or "the works of William Shakespeare."

"Good works" appears in Ephesians 2:10 (KJV), a familiar verse to most Christians:

> *For we are his workmanship, created in Christ Jesus unto good works, which God hath before ordained that we should walk in them.*

Here we find useful insights into how our "good works" help us bear fruit for Jesus Christ. The Greek word *poiema,* translated as "workmanship" here, also means "craft," or "product." The NLT goes so far as to say we are God's "masterpiece." I believe Paul was using this term to help the Ephesian Gentile trade workers, those who had given up their jobs in the Temple of Artemis, to understand the true difference between faith and works. These people had come from a lifestyle where their status in society was largely based on how much work they put into the Temple or into creating artifacts for pagan worship. Paul said in Ephesians 2:8–9 [my paraphrase], "We're saved by grace, through faith, which itself is a gift from God, and not of works, lest anyone might boast about having achieved it on their own." It was a radical departure from their former perspective.

If you're like me, you've probably read Ephesians 2:10 many times with barely a passing thought about the phrase "good works": going to church, giving money, telling people about Christ, serving others, and so on.

But it means a lot more. A couple of key words in this verse lend an altogether different, specific, and much more intentional meaning to "good works." The first word is the Greek preposition *epi,* translated "unto" in the KJV, "for" in the NASB, and "to do" in the NIV. This little word, according to one Greek dictionary, has over forty different possible meanings. However, looking at how it is used with the words around it, we can find the most accurate meaning Paul originally intended. That meaning is "for the purpose of." Writing to the Ephesian Gentile trade workers who used to take pride in their pagan temple works of craftsmanship, Paul is telling them we are God's work of craftsmanship, created for the purpose of doing our own good works.

The second key word here is *proeitomaisen,* which literally means to "prepare in advance" or "make ready beforehand." According to several commentators, this word indicates specific rather than general preparations. Paul is talking about good works that are directly and individually tailored for each of us. In the terminology he used with the Ephesian trade workers, they are specific construction jobs or projects God has prepared in advance for us to do, or more literally, to "walk in them." Consider it this way: God is the owner of His fields and has decided to engage the work of laborers, you and me, to help Him bring in the harvest. He actually created and equipped each of us to perform specific tasks in His great harvest.

I hope you see by now that the Bible says little about how to choose a particular job or compare one decision alternative to another. On the other hand, it says quite a lot about how to conduct ourselves on the job we have. It says much about how we should frame the context of every decision we make. We are told to work hard and to be good stewards of the gifts, talents, interests, and circumstances God has given us. We are told to strengthen ourselves and grow the fruit of the Spirit in our own lives so we can recognize when He is giving us a specific project in His field and respond to the needs of those around us. We are told to learn how to discern His truth against Satan's lies.

Like a wise and caring land owner, God has lined up a series of "good works" for each of His laborers, projects and tasks to be completed in order to cultivate and bring in the harvest. These projects might include going to school, learning a trade, becoming good at our jobs, and wisely managing our affairs, while remaining sensitive to the needs of those He brings into our path. We may have made plans that were derailed by a sickness, an injury, a lost job, or a divorce. God isn't surprised or unaware that these things have happened. He tells us to look for His new project assignments in these circumstances. Like Joseph in the jail, or Jonah in the whale, these new assignments are sacred opportunities God brings our way to fulfill His ultimate plan. At the same time, they are opportunities to help those around us, as Paul said in Titus 3:14, to "meet the pressing needs so that [we] will not be unfruitful."

You may be familiar with James 2:14, which says, "What good is it, my brothers, if a man claims to have faith but has no deeds [works]? Can such faith save him?" James answers this question in verse 17, "In the same way, faith by itself, if it is not accompanied by action, is dead." When Peter said in 2 Peter 1:5–7, "add to your faith moral courage and to moral courage knowledge" he ended the list with love. Paul listed love first when he listed, in Galatians 5:22, the fruits of the spirit. He said in 1 Corinthians 13:2 that if he had faith to move mountains but did not have love, he was nothing. In the next verse, he said that if he gave away everything he had to the poor or even burned himself at the stake, and did not have love, it would produce no benefit. We are told seven times in the New Testament that loving our neighbor as ourselves fulfills the law and prophets. Remember what Jesus said in Matthew 22:37–40:

"Love the Lord your God with all your heart and with all your soul and with all your mind."

This is the first and greatest commandment.

And the second is like it: "Love your neighbor as yourself."

All the Law and the Prophets hang on these two commandments.

Most Christians are familiar with Hebrews 10:25, which encourages us to "not give up meeting together." It is the proof text pastors rely on to encourage people to come to church. But have you looked at the verse right before it? Hebrews 10:24 may be one of the most understated verses in the Bible: "And let us consider how we may spur one another on toward love and good deeds." The word "consider" here comes from the root word *noeoh*, which means "to direct one's mind" or "examine carefully." The word "spur" comes from the Greek *paroxusmon*, from which we get the word "paroxysm." That word means "convulsion" or "outburst." Here's my own paraphrase of this verse, "Let's leave no stone unturned, looking for every possible way to provoke outbursts of God's love and His good works in each other!"

You are probably familiar with the story of the Good Samaritan in Luke 10:25–37, where a lawyer tried to lure Jesus into a semantic trap by asking Him what he needed to do to gain eternal life. Jesus asked him how he interpreted the law on this question. The lawyer said the same thing Jesus had spoken in Matthew 22:37–39, "Love the Lord your God with all your heart, soul, strength, and mind, and love your neighbor as yourself." Jesus said, "You're right, do this and you'll live." Then the lawyer sprung his trap, "And, ladies and gentlemen of the jury, just who is my neighbor?" Jesus, in response, told the story of a man who'd been traveling and was beaten and robbed by bandits. The man was lying on the side of the road, bloody and bruised. A Jewish priest and a Levite, a card-carrying member of the priestly tribe of Israel, each saw him and walked on by. Then a Samaritan, who belonged to a group of people the Jews hated and avoided at all costs, found the man and checked him into a hotel, doctored his wounds and told the hotel manager to let him stay until he got better. The Samaritan told the manager to charge his account if the man needed anything else.

"Who was this man's neighbor?" Jesus asked. The lawyer said, "The one who showed mercy." Jesus told him to go and do likewise, and the lawyer promptly disappeared from the pages of Scripture. But the lesson lives on as a demonstration of how far we should be willing to go to show love and good works. May we "Christians-as-farmers" leave no stone unturned to provoke such outbursts in each other.

DOES GOD WANT US TO BE RICH?

Unfortunately, many people follow God in a hope to get rich, to prosper materially through His blessings. Quite a few churches today fully embrace the idea that God's will is to give earthly riches to those who are truly committed to Him. Many Christians "pray and play" the lottery hoping God will answer their prayers and let them win some big bucks. Others, at the other end of the spectrum, work eighty-plus hours a week, sacrificing their health and their families in order to get rich. I worked with these people for years in the software industry, in companies that are run by some of the richest people on the planet. These twenty-first century tycoons can afford any luxury they want but they are subject to the same spiritual laws as the rest of us.

Christian author Randy Alcorn tells a powerful story about John D. Rockefeller, one of the richest men who ever lived, who made his fortune in the oil business over one hundred years ago at the beginning of the automotive age. When Rockefeller died, someone asked his accountant, "How much money did John D. Rockefeller leave behind?"

The accountant replied, "All of it."

When today's billionaires die, they will likely have extravagant and well-attended funerals. But, as an old Texas preacher said, "I've never seen a U-Haul trailer towed behind a hearse!" The ancient Egyptians buried the pharaohs with their favorite worldly possessions so they might be able to enjoy them in the afterlife. The possessions didn't make it. Instead, they stayed behind in the tombs to be dug up by thieves or collected by archeologists and put on display in museums. Remember the bumper sticker that said, "He who dies with the most toys wins"? A Christian bumper sticker said in response, "He who dies with the most toys wins—nothing!" What's the point of being rich when, rich and poor alike, we depart this world with as many possessions as we brought into it? The Bible says in Mark 8:36, "What shall it profit a man if he shall gain the whole world and lose his own soul?"

In Proverbs 23:4–5, Solomon, the richest man ever, said, "Do not wear yourself out to get rich; have the wisdom to show restraint. Cast but a glance at riches, and they are gone, for they will surely sprout wings and fly off to the sky like an eagle." There's an interesting passage in Jeremiah 22:13–16, where God is talking about Jehoiakim, an evil king of Judah, who was the son of Josiah, a good king. God says:

> *Woe to him who builds his palace by unrighteousness, his upper rooms by injustice, making his countrymen work for nothing, not paying them for their labor.*

> *He says, "I will build myself a great palace with spacious upper rooms." So he makes large windows in it, panels it with cedar and decorates it in red.*

> *Does it make you a king to have more and more cedar?*

> *Did not your father have food and drink? He did what was right and just, so all went well with him. He defended the cause of the poor and needy, and so all went well. Is that not what it means to know me?*

Jehoiakim plotted and schemed, abusing the people to build his lavish palaces. Does this sound familiar? How many people today, especially those in leadership positions of politics or business, abuse those who work for them in order to get to the top? This doesn't impress God at all. Jeremiah 22:15 in the NLT says, "But a beautiful cedar palace does not make a great king." Take note of the striking question God asks in verse 16: "Defending the cause of the poor and needy, isn't that what it means to know me?" In Isaiah 1:23, God told Israel how unimpressed He was with those who had achieved power and status:

> *Your rulers are rebels, companions of thieves; they all love bribes and chase after gifts.*

They do not defend the cause of the fatherless; the widow's case does not come before them.

Think about it: these people were the kings and rulers of God's chosen nation. Wouldn't they have achieved some kind of special status with Him? As I write this, Wall Street has recently gone through a historic financial meltdown. CEOs and financial managers, along with their politician enablers, have driven companies into the ground while they've walked away with bonuses and golden parachutes worth tens of millions of dollars. All this while their employees and clients have lost everything. I can't help but believe God will one day ask them the same questions He asked Jehoiakim.

Today's business news is full of stories about corporate executives who've achieved major success by laying off entire divisions of employees, scoring big points with Wall Street and bigger paychecks for themselves. These executives run roughshod over their people to make a couple of extra points of profit margin for the quarterly reports, unconcerned or unaware of the hidden costs they've incurred in lost morale, disrupted homes, and broken lives. The first line in their annual report or stock prospectus often says, "Our people are our most important asset." In the next sentence, they take pride in their "hard-nosed business acumen," destroying careers, homes, and livelihoods in order to tidy up the balance sheet for a higher stock price or an easier and more profitable corporate sale. Worse yet, as we see in the newspaper almost every day, far too many of them lie and cheat to make those numbers.

Proverbs 21:6 says, "Wealth created by lying is a vanishing mist and a deadly trap."

Is it wrong to be rich? No, it's not wrong. It's just a lot more dangerous because it cuts to the core of our fallen human nature, our pride and our fleshly greed. Proverbs 30:7–9 highlights this problem:

Two things I ask of you, O Lord; do not refuse me before I die: Keep falsehood and lies far from me; give me neither poverty nor riches, but give me only my daily bread.

Otherwise, I may have too much and disown you and say, "Who is the Lord?" Or I may become poor and steal, and so dishonor the name of my God.

God is not impressed with earthly riches. They are tools to accomplish good works or evil ones. God will hold us accountable for how we use them. They are certainly not a characteristic of a godly life unless they are required for the specific projects and tasks He has given us.

There's another problem: this line of thinking, "Don't seek after worldly riches" is used by too many Christians as an excuse to not work hard, to kick back and take the path of least resistance. Many times in my years as a Christian, I have seen people choose the easier path, making excuses for failure—or failure to even try—by saying, "Well, God doesn't want me to be one of those corporate 'muckety-mucks.'" They'll say, "I'm just a poor, humble servant for the Lord, so I'm going to sit here and be content with what little I have and not try for that promotion or learn that new skill." They'll quote 1 Timothy 6:6–8:

But godliness with contentment is great gain.

For we brought nothing into the world, and we can take nothing out of it.

But if we have food and clothing, we will be content with that.

And, of course, they'll be sure to quote the world-famous passage that comes a few verses later, in 1 Timothy 6:10:

For the love of money is a root of all kinds of evil. Some people, eager for money, have wandered from the faith and pierced themselves with many griefs.

Paul repeated these thoughts in Hebrews 13:5:

Keep your lives free from the love of money and be content with what you have, because God has said, "Never will I leave you; never will I forsake you."

Using these verses as their proof, they'll say it's more spiritual to be poor. Paul didn't say "money is the root of all kinds of evil." He said "the love of money" is. Look closely and you'll see there are no passive words in these verses or, especially, the ones that follow afterward in 1 Timothy 6:11–12:

> But you [Timothy], man of God, flee from all this [chasing after money], and pursue righteousness, godliness, faith, love, endurance and gentleness [which is "composure" or "strength under control"].

> Fight the good fight of the faith. Take hold of the eternal life to which you were called when you made your good confession in the presence of many witnesses.

Yes, those who go after the money get off God's track and run into trouble, and Paul told Timothy to run away from the false promise of worldly riches. But he also instructed him to *chase* after the list of character traits that, not surprisingly, are the same fruits of the spirit listed in Galatians 5:22 and "these things" in 2 Peter 1:5–7. He told him to *fight* the good fight of the faith, like a boxer in a ring, and *grab hold* of the eternal life to which he's been called. This doesn't sound like the approach many "poor, humble servants" adopt, which is to expend the least amount of energy while taking the path of least resistance.

Did you notice Paul never said we should not be rich? No, in 1 Timothy 6:17–19 he gave specific advice to those who are:

> Command those who are rich in this present world not to be arrogant nor to put their hope in wealth, which is so uncertain, but to put their hope in God, who richly provides us with everything for our enjoyment.

> Command them to do good, to be rich in good deeds, and to be generous and willing to share.

> In this way they will lay up treasure for themselves as a firm foundation for the coming age, so that they may take hold of the life that is truly life.

If God leads you or me to a particular project or task in His field that brings financial gain, our responsibility is to be rich in good works and to be good stewards of what God has provided: wise, generous, and willing to share with others. Jesus said in Luke 6:38, "Give and it will be given to you. A good measure, pressed down, shaken together and running over, will be poured into your lap. For with the measure you use, it will be measured to you." When Paul said to be content with what we have, he did not mean that we should stop trying for more. He meant that our focus is to be on God's projects, His missions, and not on the tools He gives us to accomplish the

God is going to lead people to execute missions in places of wealth and power. Like Joseph as prime minister of Egypt, He expects them to carry out those missions with wisdom and compassion. One of Satan's most effective schemes is designed to take Christians out of key roles in the world around us. Some church leaders believe Christians should not occupy positions of influence in business or government. If godly Christians won't stand up and take those roles, who will? There's a mission to go into these fields, cultivate them and bring in a harvest for God rather than leave the ground, untended, to the devil. The false modesty of the "poor, humble, uneducated servant" doesn't impress Him. This is an issue of stewardship: think of the things a godly, morally courageous and self-controlled Christian, responsibly holding a position of wealth or leadership, can do to better the lives of those around him or her. Far too often, the roles will fall to those, like King Jehoiakim, whose god is their own desires, those who are willing to destroy homes and livelihoods in their prideful quest for earthly power and riches.

It's not wrong to be in those corporate "muckety-muck" positions; it is wrong to be there and focused on the wrong things. Paul said in Ephesians 5:11, "And have no fellowship with the unfruitful works of darkness, but rather reprove them."

Finally, note the word "enjoyment" in 1 Timothy 6:17. This is as valid a promise as any other in Scripture. God will richly provide us with all things to enjoy. I find it interesting that Paul wrote this from prison. Talk about a different set of priorities! Later, he told Timothy that the farmer is to be the first to enjoy the fruits of his harvest. You have to wonder how much God had changed Paul's heart for him to say this from jail. God is not only inviting us to be part of His harvest of the ages, He is interested in our well-being. Unless it suits His higher purposes, He will not give us a life only of suffering, denial and hardship. Yes, He told us we'll have that, but alongside will come seasons of blessings, of abundance, relief and enjoyment.

A HARVEST OF RIGHTEOUSNESS AND PEACE

A little book in the Old Testament powerfully illustrates how God works with us through the "Christian-as-farmer" perspective. It beautifully demonstrates how God's training program of discipline brings about the harvest of righteousness and peace. The Book of Ruth is a story of love, second chances, good stewardship, and redemption. It is the story of Naomi, a fairly well-known Jewish woman from the town of Bethlehem, her Gentile daughter-in-law Ruth, and Naomi's close relative by marriage, Boaz. If you've read the book, you know a famine had broken out in the land of Israel. Because of Israel's sin, God chose not to bring the rain, causing the crops to die. There was no harvest, and consequently, no food. In response, Naomi went with her husband and two sons to live in the country of Moab, about fifty miles away.

Moab had a significant and decidedly unfavorable history with the children of Israel. Numbers 22 and 23 tell the story of Balaam, a "soothsayer," who was co-opted by the king of Moab to pronounce a curse on Israel. The Moabites worshipped a false god, Chemosh, who is called an abomination almost every time he's mentioned in the Old Testament. Moab had refused to give food and water to the children of Israel when they were in the desert wilderness on the way to the Promised Land. The Israelite men indulged in sexual immorality with the Moabite women (Numbers 25:1). Because of this sordid history, God instructed the Israelites in Deuteronomy 23:3 to not let a Moabite man into the congregation of Israel to the tenth generation. In verse 6, they were warned not to enter into a treaty of friendship with them.

Let's just say that Naomi's husband, Elimelech, whose name ironically means "my God is king," sent a strong message to the Lord God of Israel when he took his wife and two sons into this land of false gods to find food. Think about Paul's warnings in 1 Corinthians 10. Elimelech essentially mocked God by saying, "I don't believe you can provide for me, so I'll go to Moab and put my trust in Chemosh, whom you consider an abomination." God eventually judged Elimelech's idolatrous disobedience and took his life. After he died, Naomi stayed in Moab long enough for her two sons to marry local women. God judged the two sons, who apparently were also comfortable in this land of false gods, by taking their lives. Shortly thereafter, Naomi, who was living with her two Moabite daughters-in-law, heard that the famine in Israel was over and decided to move home. One of her daughters-in-law chose to stay in Moab, but Ruth, the other, decided to leave her home, her family, and her god to follow Naomi back to Bethlehem.

There are a couple of things to realize about the decision Naomi and Ruth made to go back to Bethlehem. Naomi told Ruth there wouldn't be any family inheritance for her if she came to Israel. In Ruth 1:13, she told her daughters-in-law that life would be harsher for her than either of them, because "the Lord has raised His hand against me." This reminds me of the image I used to have of God, sitting up there in His heavenly rocking chair, waiting to back-hand me upside the head whenever I did something wrong. I can almost hear Naomi saying, "Girls, stay here in Moab, go find yourself another husband and have a good life. Don't come back to Bethlehem with me. God has smacked me upside the head and will probably do it again a few more times."

Ruth, as a Gentile foreigner or "stranger" living in Bethlehem, had few rights and almost no social standing among the people of Israel. Even so, she evidently had heard enough about the Lord God of Israel from her in-laws that she decided it was worth leaving her family and her pagan gods in Moab to follow Him.

Naomi, upon her return to Bethlehem after ten years, met her old friends and told them to call her Mara, or "bitter," because the Lord had dealt so bitterly with her. Imagine her situation: she had obeyed her husband and followed him into Moab during the famine. She probably knew it was a bad idea and would not end well. But after he died, she stayed, essentially enabling her two sons to plant roots in Moab. Now Naomi was bitter at God for the difficult set of circumstances in which she found herself, saying in Ruth 1:21 that He has "testified against me and afflicted me."

I'm reminded again of Proverbs 19:3 (NLT), "People ruin their lives by their own foolishness and then are angry at the Lord." You may think I'm being a bit harsh on Naomi: you should see what some of the commentators wrote about her! The key point is this: we need to realize how seriously God takes our desire, or lack thereof, to trust in Him and His ability to provide for us, especially if we turn to false gods for that provision.

We don't know the effect Naomi's bitter response had on Ruth's view of her new God and her new homeland. We do know Ruth demonstrated her *commitment* to God by leaving Moab to accompany Naomi back to Israel. Then she demonstrated her *obedience* to Him as soon as she arrived. What did Ruth do? She went out to pick grain in the fields so she and Naomi could eat.

As we noted earlier, God may not tell us a lot of things, but He has clearly told us to get out there and work for our food. In Ruth's and Naomi's day, the people of Israel had a law that provided food for the poor and foreigners living among them. It was called "gleaning," and is described in Leviticus 19:9–10. The harvesters of the crops were to "round off" the corners of the fields, leaving ripened grain in the corners for the poor. They were instructed to leave behind any grain that was not picked as they harvested, called the "gleanings," lying in the fields for the poor. But the poor were told to go into the fields and pick the grain. They were not excused from God's principle of working for their food.

Ruth 2:2–3 contains an excellent example of how God expects us to do certain things as we work for our food, while only He can do others. Ruth took the only job available to her as a newly arrived Gentile foreigner in

Bethlehem. She went out and found a field where she could pick some grain. Verse 3 reveals where God stepped in and did His part:

So she went out and began to glean in the fields behind the harvesters.

As it turned out, she found herself working in a field belonging to Boaz, who was from the clan of Elimelech.

"As it turned out, she found herself ... " The KJV says "and her hap was to ... " and the NASB says "she happened to" start working in the field belonging to Boaz. As one of the commentators said, "I can imagine the angels of heaven holding their breath, waiting to see if she would actually stop in Boaz's field." Personally, I'd think the angels had a much more involved and proactive role than that. Maybe they were whispering in her ear, "This way, Ruth! The field you're standing in looks kind of puny, huh? How about that one over there? It looks much better, doesn't it, Ruth?"

I'm reminded of a wonderful man I sat next to at a recent conference who quoted Proverbs 16:9 to me, "In his heart a man plans his course, but the Lord determines his steps." The timing and circumstances of this chance encounter made me realize how precisely God can line up events to accomplish His will. Who knows how, but God obviously planned and orchestrated events such that Ruth would end up gleaning in Boaz's field. She merely set out to glean in any field where she could find grain and be reasonably safe. God, at the same time, determined her steps by leading her to the field of Boaz, which opened up a whole new set of opportunities—and missions with eternal consequences. She was doing her part, and God was doing His.

Ruth 2:1 says Boaz was a "man of standing." The KJV says he was "a mighty man of wealth." As one commentator stated, the Hebrew words here indicate a combination of wealth, social status, and valor. Apparently Boaz was a warrior, a man of respected position and a possessor of substantial wealth. He was clearly a good and decent man who honored God with his stewardship and maintained good relations with his employees. In Ruth 2:4, we see he took the time to greet his harvesters and they responded well to his greeting. No patronizing, greedy, or austere employer and no sulking, surly employees. All through chapters 2 and 3, we see how well Boaz took care of his employees by providing them shelter and water as they worked in his fields. We also see, however, that he kept a firm hand on them by clearly instructing them how to treat Ruth as she gleaned among them.

Some commentators say that when Boaz first saw Ruth, it was love at first sight. What I see instead in chapters 2 and 3 is a godly man, living in ungodly times, who took seriously God's instructions to help the poor, widows, and fatherless among them. He undoubtedly knew in his heart what his great-great grandson Solomon would write years later in Proverbs 19:17 (KJV):

> *"He that hath pity upon the poor lendeth unto the Lord; and that which he hath given will he pay him again."*

Boaz was aware that Ruth was Naomi's daughter-in-law, and he knew Naomi was his own close relative by marriage. He undoubtedly knew that God had judged the land around Bethlehem with famine because of Israel's disobedience during that time (see Judges 21:25). He saw the bounty of his own harvest coming from the hand of the Lord and would be sure to honor Him accordingly. He could have schemed on his own to take advantage of Ruth by marrying her or, as is implied by some, having sexual relations with her. But those things did not happen. He made it possible for her to work in more comfortable conditions than she could expect as a poor, foreign widow gleaning in any other field of Bethlehem. I believe Boaz's intentions indicate his desire to please God, as is plain from Ruth 2:11–12:

> *Boaz replied, "I've been told all about what you have done for your mother-in-law since the death of your husband—how you left your father and mother and your homeland and came to live with a people you did not know before.*

"May the Lord repay you for what you have done. May you be richly rewarded by the Lord, the God of Israel, under whose wings you have come to take refuge."

The Bible says in Ruth 2:23 that she worked in Boaz's fields through the barley and wheat harvests, which lasted about six weeks from late April to early June, and lived with Naomi during that time. Boaz treated her as one of his "servant girls," and although he was treating her well, he still expected her to work. Ruth was grateful she could work and provide food for herself and her mother-in-law. Even though Naomi recognized right away that Ruth was working in the field of a kinsman-redeemer, it apparently took her several weeks to consider Boaz as a potential husband for her daughter-in-law. The Law of Moses came into the picture again, providing for the family of a deceased man who had died without any sons to carry on his family name. According to Deuteronomy 25:5–10, one of his brothers or close relatives would be required to serve the role of kinsman redeemer, marrying the deceased man's wife so that she could have sons through him and carry on her first husband's name and tribal inheritance.

Ruth 3:1 says that one day Naomi advised Ruth to dress up and approach Boaz late that night at the threshing floor, a place where they separated the grain from the chaff, and uncover his feet. This was essentially the way a woman could propose to a man under Jewish law and claim his financial and hereditary protection as the *goel*, the kinsman redeemer. Doing this at night in a somewhat private place, according to many of the commentators, would give Boaz an opportunity to accept or reject this offer without losing face in the community.

Ruth agreed to do everything Naomi said, and went to the big "threshing party" that Boaz, like any landowner of his day celebrating a successful harvest, would throw for the workers. After the party was over, Boaz and his workers would go to sleep around the piles of grain to protect them from thieves. Ruth waited until everyone had gone to sleep and discreetly approached Boaz. She uncovered his feet and lay there. He awoke, startled to find her at his feet. At this point she used some specific terminology, saying to him, "Spread your skirt over me," indicating the proposal of marriage as a kinsman redeemer. Boaz praised her virtuous character and promised to exercise his role as the kinsman redeemer. Ruth chapter 4 tells how he successfully exercised the role over another relative who was a nearer kinsman than he. At this point, he was able to marry Ruth and father a child with her, a son named Obed, who became the grandfather of King David and an ancestor of *Yeshua Ha'Mashiach*, the Messiah of Israel.

Much is made in the commentaries and sermons about how this lovely book is a picture of Christ and the church, how the kinsman redeemer loved and married the Gentile bride. Often overlooked in the story is the beautiful redemption of Naomi and her second chance to receive blessings from the hand of God. Here was someone who had experienced severe tests through God's rigorously applied training program of discipline, in His effort to bring her back from following after false gods to meet her material needs. Here was someone who repented, came back into Israel to live according to God's rules, and accepted the consequences of her past decisions in order to restore herself to fellowship with Him.

God didn't permanently cast Naomi aside, put her on a shelf, or give her the last-place prize outside of the bull's-eye. Instead, He used her to fulfill a key part of His ultimate plan and blessed her with a grandson whom she was able to personally nurse and nurture. The women of Bethlehem praised God for rewarding Naomi with a daughter-in-law "who loves you and is better than seven sons." She got to enjoy the first fruits of her harvest here on earth through her grandson. She will undoubtedly enjoy for eternity her reward in God's ultimate plan as an ancestor of King David and the Lord Jesus Christ.

I'm sure Naomi would agree with the promising words of Hebrews 12:11:

> *No discipline seems pleasant at the time, but painful. Later on, however, it produces a harvest of righteousness and peace for those who have been trained by it.*

The Greek word *karpos,* translated here as "harvest" and as "fruit" in the KJV, is used in many places in the Bible to indicate the end result of a farmer's labors and the season of growth. This phrase, "the harvest of peace and righteousness," also appears in Isaiah 32:17 and James 3:18. It means that the end result of our endeavors, the outcome of our missions of labor in God's field, is freedom from worry about our alignment with the will of God.

Isn't that what you and I are looking for?

THE SACRIFICE

In 2 Timothy 2:11, Paul said, "Here is a trustworthy saying: If we died with him, we will also live with him." This gives us insight into the fourth perspective of the victorious Christian life God has given to "the rest of us." It is the role of a sacrifice, the taking of an innocent life to cover the sins of another. Jesus Christ on the cross, the ultimate and sufficient sacrifice of all time, is the bedrock foundation of our Christian beliefs, the essence of our stewardship, and the basis of our hope in eternal life. For me, it calls to mind Galatians 2:20:

> I have been crucified with Christ and I no longer live, but Christ lives in me. The life I live in the body, I live by faith in the Son of God, who loved me and gave himself for me.

"God's will," the Christian experience, is fundamentally linked not only to the sacrifice Jesus Christ made for us on the cross, but also to our responsibility to give our lives back to Him. It's directly aligned with the fulfillment of Old Testament laws and prophecies about "atonement," the payment for sin by offering an innocent sacrifice.

ALTARS, SACRIFICES AND TEMPLES

If you've been a Christian for any length of time, you probably know Romans 12:1–2:

> *Therefore, I urge you, brothers, in view of God's mercy, to offer your bodies as living sacrifices, holy and pleasing to God—this is your spiritual act of worship.*
>
> *Do not conform any longer to the pattern of this world, but be transformed by the renewing of your mind. Then you will be able to test and approve what God's will is—his good, pleasing and perfect will.*

This familiar passage contains a treasure of promises and blessings. For starters, it says we can "test and approve" God's will. What does this mean? The Greek word used for "test and approve" is *dokimazo*, which means to prove something that has a certain outcome. It reminds me of the math and science classes I took years ago in engineering school when I had to "prove" mathematical theorems or chemical formulas. These proofs were exercises in logic because, once the correct conditions were put in place, the results were always the same. They are based on the laws of physics, which are predictable and consistent. Similarly, God's will is something we prove, because we can expect a certain outcome if we set up and follow the correct guidelines. It is based on the moral laws of the universe which God has set up. From our earthly perspective, they may not seem quite as consistent but from His vantage point are equally predictable.

As we saw earlier, the words "good, pleasing, and perfect" in Romans 12:2 are adjectives, not nouns: God's will *is* good, pleasing, and perfect, not three different rings around a bull's-eye. They are the characteristics of God's will we can experience when we present our bodies to Him as a living sacrifice. God's good, pleasing and perfect will is the certain outcome when we make the effort to conform to His Word and not the social mores of this present world.

What does it mean to offer ourselves as a living sacrifice? Why did Paul use this picture? Although we may be unfamiliar with his references to temples and sacrifices, Paul's first-century audience knew what he was talking about. Temples and sacrifices on altars were a major part of life in his time for Jews and Gentiles alike. Anyone who's been to Greece or Rome has seen the ancient temples that were built as places to worship pagan gods. Historians tell us the Temple to Artemis (Diana) in Ephesus was the cultural center of the entire region of Asia. The practices of temple worship and offerings of sacrifices have mostly passed into history, but they still carry enormous significance for you and me as we try to understand and follow God's will for our lives.

The Bible first mentions a sacrifice on an altar in Genesis 8:20. When Noah and his family climbed out of the ark after the great flood, he offered "some of all the clean animals and birds" as a sacrifice to God, and the Lord "smelled the pleasing aroma." God made a covenant with Noah to never again destroy all living creatures as He had in the flood. The Lord gave Noah instructions about man's changed relationship with the animals, specifically mentioning the importance of the lifeblood. According to Genesis 9:4–6, God would require an "accounting of the lifeblood" of every man and animal.

After the flood, Noah and his family followed God's instruction to multiply and repopulate the earth. Many years later, God revealed Himself to Abraham and promised He'd make him the father of a chosen nation. Abraham's descendents, through his son Isaac and grandson Jacob, became the nation of Israel. Still later, God revealed His Law to Moses. A fundamental part of the Law included regular and frequent sacrifices of innocent animals to the Lord as atonement for the sins of the people of Israel. The concept of animal sacrifice took on a central part of their daily lives.

God gave Moses a set of detailed instructions to build a large and elaborate tent called the Tabernacle, a central place to offer the sacrifices. God's instructions to Moses spelled out how it was to be assembled, disassembled, and carried from place to place as the children of Israel wandered in the wilderness. His instructions also described the ritual ceremonies that the priests from the tribe of Levi would conduct each day and on special "feast" days throughout the year.

If you or I were living in Israel during Old Testament times and went to the Tabernacle, we'd see the priests offering sacrifices in the mornings and evenings according to a precise ritual. A male animal would be chosen, without spot or blemish; it would be washed, placed on the altar in a specific way, and killed. Its lifeblood would be sprinkled on the altar in an exact pattern. The priest chosen for that day's duties would offer incense on the table in the Holy Place and pray to God to forgive the sins of the people.

For almost five hundred years, from the time of Moses to the time of David, this ritual was performed in the Tabernacle, which was intended to be a temporary, portable structure until the Jews settled in the Promised Land. In 1 Chronicles 17, David asked God to let him build a permanent house, a Temple in Jerusalem, where the sacrifices could be made in one place to the Lord each day. God responded that David would not be the one to build His house. Instead, the mission would go to David's son, Solomon.

When he finished building the grand and beautiful Temple, Solomon was overpowered by the magnitude of what God had instructed Him to do. He asked in 2 Chronicles 5:18, "But will God really dwell on earth with men? The heavens, even the highest heavens, cannot contain you. How much less this temple I have built!" Nevertheless, the expectation of Old Testament Jews was that God would physically dwell in the building, in the innermost chamber called the "Holy of Holies" and physically meet with the High Priest once a year on the Day of Atonement.

With the exception of the Babylonian captivity, the Temple in Jerusalem served as the central place of Jewish sacrificial worship for almost nine hundred years. There were actually two Temples; the first one built by Solomon was destroyed when the Babylonians sacked Jerusalem over five hundred years before Christ. It was rebuilt by Zerubbabel as described in the book of Ezra. King Herod of Rome restored and significantly expanded it shortly before Christ was born. This Second Temple was destroyed by General Titus Vespasian and his Roman legions in 70 AD. Some Jews today anticipate the day when a Third Temple is built and animal sacrifices are reinstated.

When Paul wrote his letters to the New Testament Christians, the daily animal sacrifices were still being conducted in the Second Temple. However, something quite interesting happened just prior to that, around 30 AD. When Jesus of Nazareth was crucified on the cross outside Jerusalem, the thick curtain separating the Holy of Holies from the rest of the Temple's inner chamber was ripped completely in half, from top to bottom. This miraculous event signified what Paul explained in Ephesians 2:11–16: God has brought Jews and Gentiles together through the blood of Christ, "by abolishing in his flesh the law with its commandments and regulations" (verse 15).

If you read Paul's New Testament letters closely, you see that a group of Jews, called Judaizers, were following him from church to church trying to "reconvert" new Christians back to strict obedience of the Jewish law. These were the same people he warned Titus about, those who would ruin entire households for personal gain, whether power or wealth. In virtually all of his letters, Paul pointed out to both Jews and Gentiles how Jesus Christ fulfilled the Law and why strict obedience to it was no longer necessary. The animal sacrifices were abolished because Jesus Christ became the ultimate sacrifice for all time. In Hebrews 9, Paul explained how God's New Testament, His new legal contract with His people, literally transfers jurisdiction of sin's atonement from the Temple rituals to Jesus Christ's death, burial, and resurrection. In particular, Hebrews 9:11–12 describes this major shift in God's ultimate plan:

When Christ came as high priest of the good things that are already here, he went through the greater and more perfect tabernacle that is not man-made, that is to say, not a part of this creation.

He did not enter by means of the blood of goats and calves; but he entered the Most Holy Place once for all by his own blood, having obtained eternal redemption.

God, for His own purposes, ordained the elaborate Old Testament sacrificial system to point us to *Ha'Mashiach*, the Messiah who would take away the sins of the world. This is our complete redemption in Jesus Christ. The Law alone could not accomplish such complete redemption. As Hebrews 10:1–4 explains:

The law is only a shadow of the good things that are coming—not the realities themselves. For this reason it can never, by the same sacrifices repeated endlessly year after year, make perfect those who draw near to worship.

If it could, would they not have stopped being offered? For the worshipers would have been cleansed once for all, and would no longer have felt guilty for their sins.

But those sacrifices are an annual reminder of sins, because it is impossible for the blood of bulls and goats to take away sins.

This passage makes clear how inadequate "the blood of bulls and goats," the Old Testament laws and sacrificial rituals, were to fully atone for our sins. In Galatians 3:24–25 (KJV), Paul told this group of believers, whom the Judaizers had convinced to return to the Old Testament practices:

Wherefore the law was our schoolmaster to bring us unto Christ, that we might be justified by faith.

But after that faith is come, we are no longer under a schoolmaster.

The word translated "schoolmaster" is the Greek word *paidagogous*, from which we get our word "pedagogue." Today, this is another word for a teacher. The commentators tell us it originally referred not to a teacher but to a slave who used to accompany a young upper-class boy to and from school, keeping him focused on his studies. The slave served as a combination tutor, guardian, and companion to the boy. Once Christ offered Himself as the ultimate sacrifice, Paul said in verse 24, the tutor was no longer needed.

How significant is this for us?

When God dwelled in the Holy of Holies in the Temple (or Tabernacle), He required the High Priest to go through an elaborate and specific set of preparations in order to meet with Him once a year on the Day of Atonement. There is a Jewish legend that the High Priest went behind the curtain into the Holy of Holies with bells sewed to the waist of his robe (Exodus 28:33–35) and a rope tied around his leg that snaked back into the outer chamber. If the bells stopped ringing, according to the legend, those who were outside knew to pull on the rope and drag out the High Priest, because he was dead. If others went in there to get him, they'd be dead, too.

Many Christians may not appreciate what it means to have such direct access to God that would have amazed—or even killed—believers of ages past. During Old Testament times, the Spirit of God only "rested upon" certain people for specific reasons. In the New Testament age, that is all changed: God's Spirit dwells in the heart of every Christian. First Corinthians 3:16 says we are God's Temple and the Holy Spirit lives in us. Paul explained to the Gentile trade workers, in Ephesians 2:19–22, that God is using the members of His *ekklesia*, the church, to build a new Holy Temple. It is built on the foundation of the apostles and prophets, fitted together with Christ as the chief cornerstone. He explained it further in 1 Corinthians 6:19–20:

Do you not know that your body is a temple of the Holy Spirit, who is in you, whom you have received from God? You are not your own; you were bought at a price. Therefore honor God with your body.

Instead of a physical offering of bulls and goats to God, we New Testament believers make a spiritual, living offering of our bodies, that part of us still subject to the sin nature. God meets us here, directly and continually, in our bodies, the new Temple of the Holy Spirit for the church age. We are challenged to present our bodies back to Him as living sacrifices of honor and obedience. Peter mentions the same principle in 1 Peter 2:5:

"You also, like living stones, are being built into a spiritual house to be a holy priesthood, offering spiritual sacrifices acceptable to God through Jesus Christ."

Think about how much mercy and grace God has lavished on those of us who have called upon His name. You might ask why God developed such a complex, public system of Old Testament rituals in the first place, only to replace it with an individually private, spiritual practice we too often take for granted today. The Bible reminds us that these elaborate rituals were never meant to take the place of a personal relationship with Him. Many passages in Scripture emphasize that God values something else much more than ritual sacrifice: obedience.

One day, the Pharisees took Jesus to task when His disciples failed to follow the prescribed "cleansing ritual" of washing their hands before eating. In Mark 7:6–7, Jesus obliged them with His opinion of their traditions:

Isaiah was right when he prophesied about you hypocrites; as it is written: "These people honor me with their lips, but their hearts are far from me.

"They worship me in vain; their teachings are but rules taught by men."

Isn't it mind-boggling that we humans have such a tendency to get so wrapped up in the process of religion while missing its very purpose? Jesus summed it up concisely in verse 9 (KJV):

> And he said unto them, Full well ye reject the commandment of God, that ye may keep your own tradition.

A similar story is told in 1 Samuel 15. King Saul disobeyed God and failed to destroy all the plunder he and his army had taken from the Amalekites, Israel's historical enemies. Saul tried to justify his actions to Samuel, the prophet, who responded in 1 Samuel 15:22, "Does the Lord delight in burnt offerings and sacrifices as much as in obeying the voice of the Lord? *To obey is better than sacrifice* [italics mine], and to heed is better than the fat of rams."

Samuel made a serious observation in the next verse, "For rebellion is like the sin of divination [witchcraft], and arrogance like the evil of idolatry. Because you have rejected the word of the Lord, he has rejected you [Saul] as king." This is a big red warning sign to those of us who might profess to follow God but are actually following human traditions. Proverbs 21:3 reinforces this warning, "The Lord is more pleased when we do what is just and right than when we give him sacrifices." In other words, God is not impressed with ritual. He looks on the heart. David, after he repented of his adultery and murder, wrote in Psalm 51:16–17, "You do not delight in sacrifice, or I would bring it; you do not take pleasure in burnt offerings. The sacrifices of God are a broken spirit; a broken and contrite heart, O God, you will not despise." Hosea 6:6, a verse Jesus quoted twice, in Matthew 9:13 and 12:7, says, "For I desire mercy, not sacrifice, and acknowledgment of God rather than burnt offerings."

The "Christian-as-sacrifice" perspective implies obedience, which is much more than following a set of religious rituals. God wants us to give Him our lives and to be willing to put ourselves on the altar as a sacrifice, to do whatever He asks of us. Hebrews 13:15–16 says:

Through Jesus, therefore, let us continually offer to God a sacrifice of praise—the fruit of lips that confess his name.

And do not forget to do good and to share with others, for with such sacrifices God is pleased.

The Christian life is not only about obeying rules. It's about finding a deep and meaningful relationship of all-giving *agape* love with the God of the Universe who first loved us.

ACCOUNTING FOR OUR SINS

Most of us want an easy-to-follow set of rules to guide us through unfamiliar territory or help us when we're swamped with too much to do. Workers in many occupations use a checklist to carry out their daily responsibilities. When I was in the army, I scored major points with my sergeants after I came up with a daily, weekly, and monthly task list our maintenance shop could use to check off the things that needed to be done. Virtually every business grades itself using some kind of accounting scorecard. As a project manager in the software industry, I prepared weekly spreadsheets that showed status and "key performance indicators" complete with red, yellow, and green colors to highlight what was or was not going according to plan.

Not surprisingly, many Christians take the same approach to following God. If we've knocked out all of the tasks on our checklist, or if all the blocks on our scorecard are green, then we must be in God's will and doing okay. Countless sermons and Christian books picture God as some grand, cosmic accountant who maintains a constantly updated set of books on each of us and the sins we commit each day. Whenever we do something wrong, according to this line of thinking, an entry is made in the liabilities column and we break fellowship with God, finding ourselves out of His will. Consequently, all kinds of bad things start happening to us. On the flip side, if we keep our sins confessed, entries are made in the assets column, we stay in God's will and good things we call blessings take place. I don't know about you, but I came out of a religion that followed this kind of rote, daily account reconciliation with God. It was tormenting, to say the least. When I accepted Christ, I thought I was being saved from all that!

You may be familiar with Psalm 66:18 (KJV), "If I regard iniquity in my heart, the Lord will not hear me." I remember hearing this verse used as a proof text in sermons telling me I have to be purified of sin to approach God in prayer. Otherwise, my prayers will bounce off the ceiling and back onto my pointy little head. Sure, the preachers were careful to offset this harsh and exacting requirement with the comforting promise of 1 John 1:9: "If we confess our sins, he is faithful and just and will forgive us our sins and purify us from all unrighteousness." Still, they characterize this as an accounting exercise: if, and only if, you and I have confessed our sins and are current on our accounts, will God forgive us, listen to our prayers, and bless us.

Here are some thoughts that have run through my mind as I've tried to grasp this point of view: *Weren't all of my sins forgiven when I accepted Christ? If so, why do I have to keep up with a daily accounting ritual? What about the ones I don't confess? What if I've forgotten a particular sin?*

Many preachers and authors of books on God's will quote David, in Psalm 139:23–24, who apparently had similar worries when he prayed:

Search me, O God, and know my heart; test me and know my anxious thoughts.

See if there is any offensive way in me, and lead me in the way everlasting.

These folks teach that we should follow a daily ritual when we go to God in prayer, similar to filling up our car's gas tank. Some even teach that we should keep a list of the sins we've committed so that we can more readily confess them when we pray. "Keep the accounts short," they advise us. I have to admit it sounds a lot like the Pharisees in Mark 7:6–7, holding onto their traditions at the expense of following God.

Solomon asked in Proverbs 20:9, "Who can say, 'I have cleansed my heart; I am pure and free from sin'?" In the same chapter, Proverbs 20:27, he said, "The Lord's searchlight penetrates the human spirit, exposing every hidden motive." How, in our limited, fallen state, could we possibly remember every sin we've committed? How is it possible for us to know them all? I realize there have been many times when I was cruising along, fat, dumb, and happy, blissfully unaware I had caused someone to grieve or fall into sin because of my own behavior. Again, the preachers and authors say, "If you ask God to search your heart and reveal the sins you've committed, He will."

Let's stop and think about that one for a minute.

First of all, I know Christians who would rather die than have a curse word cross their lips, yet they routinely harm and even ruin others through their lies and gossip. Others would not be caught dead smoking, dancing, or going to movies, but sneak regular peeks at pornographic material on the Internet. Too many of us abuse our bodies, the Temple of the Holy Spirit, through overeating and lack of exercise. We could get into finer and finer details of accusation. It doesn't address the real issue. But the good news of all time is this: every single one of our sins, past, present, and future, was dealt with on the cross. It is now a matter of gaining victory over them in our bodies, in submission to Christ according to His "strength training program for godliness" that we examined in the Christian-as-runner section.

The book of Hebrews tells us Christ's death on the cross eliminated the Old Testament requirement to offer animal sacrifices to atone for the people's sins. Wouldn't His sufficient sacrifice also eliminate the need for you and me, New Testament believers, to keep a personal set of books on our own sins? Matthew 27:51, Mark 15:38, and Luke 23:45 describe how Christ's death on the cross ripped the thick curtain in the Temple's innermost chamber completely in two, from top to bottom. Think about it: this was God's epic statement that things would be quite different going forward.

Let's not forget about Jesus' backhanded comments in Mark 7:8–9 regarding Temple sacrifices compared to a relationship with God Himself. The Pharisees had their own accounting methods for avoiding sin down to a science, but they missed the opportunity for a personal relationship with the living Son of God when He stood right in front of them. I'm concerned that if we focus on an accounting exercise to keep ourselves in balance with God, we'll miss the full effect and greater blessings of a close, personal relationship with Him.

I believe there's a different and more effective approach to staying in a pure, submitted relationship with our Almighty God and gaining victory over sin. This one enables us to see His will accomplished in our lives—and brings His blessings. First, let's go back to Psalm 66:18 (KJV), which says, "If I regard iniquity in my heart, the Lord will not hear me." The Hebrew word *ra'it'i* used here for "regard" is not "forgot" or "failed to bring up." No, it is from a root word that means "to see," "to look upon closely," or "to gaze upon." To me, it conjures up a vision of how we might gaze upon a valuable possession, such as an old photograph of a loved one or a new toy we got for Christmas. This passage indicates a proactive state of mind, of holding sin close to our hearts and gazing fondly upon it. It means we would rather have the sins in our lives than a submitted relationship with God. The cherished sins, instead of Him, are on the throne of our hearts.

Next, let's take another look at Psalm 139:23–24. "Search me, O God ..." Here, David is not talking about gaining acceptance with God; he's talking about how to clear the path to a deeper and more intimate fellowship with Him. Finally, the Greek word used in 1 John 1:9 for "confess" is *homologomen*, literally meaning to "say the same thing." This is more about a relationship than an accounting exercise. As is so powerfully stated in Ephesians 1:3–8, 2:18, 3:12, Hebrews 4:16, 10:19–22, and 1 John 5:14–15, if we go to God in prayer as His child, in the name and power of the Lord Jesus Christ, He hears us and we are accepted before His throne. Too many Christians have been told that God is so holy He requires us to be pure to approach Him. Each of these verses emphatically says we *are* pure and holy (the word literally means "set apart for God") in Jesus Christ. We don't have to be enslaved to an accounting system, or be afraid to go to God as we are—especially after we've accepted Christ. Romans 8:15 (KJV) says:

> *For ye have not received the spirit of bondage again to fear; but ye have received the Spirit of adoption, whereby we cry, Abba, Father.*

The word "Abba" means "Daddy." When was the last time you felt like going to your accountant and calling him "Daddy"? God doesn't want us to focus on keeping short transactional accounts with Him. He doesn't require a big cleansing ritual for us to approach Him. He already took care of that. He wants us to be close enough to Him in an intimate, loving and two-way relationship that we can call Him "Daddy."

WHO'S ON THE ALTAR, WHO'S ON THE THRONE?

You might say, "Tom, what about Christians who live their lives in disobedience, or even in open, flagrant sin? Are you saying it's okay for them to do so and claim Christ's sacrifice as justification for their lifestyle?" In Romans 6:1, Paul asked a similar question: "What shall we say, then? Shall we go on sinning so that grace may increase?" He answered his own question in the next verse and brought up another interesting concept:

By no means! We died to sin; how can we live in it any longer?

What did Paul mean, "We died to sin"? He gave us the answer in Romans 6:6–7:

For we know that our old self was crucified with him so that the body of sin might be done away with, that we should no longer be slaves to sin—because anyone who has died has been freed from sin.

Since we've died to sin and Jesus Christ redeemed us from the curse of the law, according to Galatians 3:13, we no longer need to keep score in a set of books. Instead, we need to keep our *position* in an intimate, submitted relationship with the God of the Universe. How does this work? For me, it means we can cut through the accounting ledgers and legal checklists and ask a far simpler question:

Who's on the altar, and who's on the throne?

A sacrifice has no will of its own—it is *dead*, completely given over to the purpose of the offering. Paul said he was crucified with Christ, but he still lived through Christ, who was living within him. He'd completely given up his own will to the Lord. He reinforced this concept in the verse we looked at in the beginning of this section, 2 Timothy 2:11, saying, "If we died with Him, we will also live with Him." God wants us to give our bodies, our sin nature, to Him so our minds can be transformed by His sanctifying work in us. By offering ourselves in submission (which, remember, means "subordinated to the mission") to His ultimate plan, we open ourselves up for the specific mission assignments and training lessons He wants to give us. Come what may, we prove His will for our lives. This is not an accounting exercise; it's a life-altering choice.

When we became Christians, we were released from the bondage of sin and made alive to Jesus Christ. Paul described this in 2 Corinthians 5:17, "Therefore, if anyone is in Christ, he is a new creation; the old has gone, the new has come." Why, then, do we continue to sin?

Now, that question has occupied theologians for centuries. In essence, it's because we're still living here on this earth in our fallen, fleshly bodies. We're subject to our own lusts, not to mention the relentless campaign of lies and deceit Satan wages against us. God has decided, for His own purposes, to constrain our full relationship with Him until we get to eternity. He uses each of the four perspectives we've studied here, as well as our physical, fleshly limitations, to refine us and train us to endure, overcome, and grow close to Him. To paraphrase 1 Peter 1:16, "It is written, be set apart for God, because I [Jesus Christ] am set apart for God." As James 1:12–16 tells us, it comes down to a choice and a practice: either we let our fleshly desires have control over us or we control them by laying them, and ourselves, on the altar, giving Him the throne of our hearts.

I learned this lesson the hard way a few years ago while I was working for a particular software company. I was laser-focused on becoming a vice president at this company, to the point that it began to affect my marriage. Kathy tried to tell me I was spending too much time on the job and coming home from my many cross-country trips worn out, angry, and bitter because things were taking too long or not going my way. Joe, my boss at the time and a very strong Christian, made an observation over lunch one day that changed my whole outlook about work. He said, "Tom, you don't work for the company, you work for the Lord."

Verses like Ephesians 6:6 and Colossians 3:22 came to mind, where Paul encourages slaves (okay, let's make the analogy to modern-day employees) to obey their masters (employers) "not with eye service as men-pleasers, but as the servants of Christ doing the will of God from the heart." Once I pulled the spear out of my heart, I began to realize I was focused on an idol, the promotion to vice president. I had to admit that I wanted this position more than I wanted God. As a result, I was doing things I thought would promote myself in the eyes of senior management and, worse, I was neglecting my marriage. Something one of my previous bosses had said years before came back, ringing in my ears:

"One wife, many jobs."

Ouch.

I realized I was wrong and went to God, not to set the accounting balances straight, but to repent and restore my intimate relationship with "Daddy," my "Abba, Father," and to tell Him that I wanted Him, not the vice president title, on the throne of my heart. I placed myself and the job on the altar as an offering to Him.

I never made vice president at that company, but got something much more valuable. I was able to strengthen my relationship with my Heavenly Father— and with my wife. When God began to prepare me for my next mission in a completely different career field, I was able to recognize the signals He was giving me and willingly leave my software career behind. I left the company for another position and took a major pay cut, almost immediately before the financial markets melted down. I had learned to put my trust in God and not the stock market or my corporate salary, so I had much less stress than before, even though the times were much worse. God met all of our financial needs and more, and continues to do so. Although Kathy and I still don't know where God will eventually lead us, we can see His hand directing our paths every day.

If you've read the book of Romans, you notice that Paul spends a lot of time explaining how we must yield ourselves completely to Jesus Christ in order to gain victory over our sinful nature. He specifically brings up this concept in Romans 6:11–12:

> In the same way, count yourselves dead to sin but alive to God in Christ Jesus. Therefore do not let sin reign in your mortal body so that you obey its evil desires.

In the next verse, Romans 6:13, Paul lays out the essential instructions for how this works:

> Do not offer the parts of your body to sin, as instruments of wickedness, but rather offer yourselves to God, as those who have been brought from death to life; and offer the parts of your body to him as instruments of righteousness.

Here is the key to Romans 12:1–2 and how we offer our bodies a living sacrifice to Him: it means exercising voluntary, deliberate acts of submission and obedience.

When we place ourselves on the altar and Him on the throne, we open ourselves to whatever He wants to do in our lives. As James 1:2–4 says, He will bring us through the tests and trials that make us mature and complete, lacking nothing. At the same time, He will open up opportunities to use us in the lives of others to bear fruit and accomplish His ultimate plan. He will even give back to us things we've given to Him.

I can tell you from personal experience that these things are much more precious when He gives them back, because they've now been set apart as holy to Him, touched by Him and returned with His blessings. Finally, as Paul told Timothy in 2 Timothy 2:12: "If we endure, we will also reign with him." This is our promise of victory through sacrifice, laying ourselves on the altar and establishing Him on the throne of our hearts.

PROVING GOD'S WILL

In our discussions of James 1:2, 12–14 and 1 Corinthians 10:13, we saw that God and Satan "test" us. We learned that the Greek word used in these passages for "test" is *peirasmos*, which means a test with an uncertain outcome. God tests us to determine whether we'll follow Him, or not. Satan tests, or tempts, us to follow our own lusts and his deceptions. James 1:2 says these tests are the ones we "happen upon" in our journey. The outcome of these tests is uncertain because it depends on our response.

On the other hand, we've seen that the root word *dokimazo,* used for "prove" in Romans 12:2, "find out" in Ephesians 5:10 and "trying" in James 1:3, means a test with a certain, definite, and positive outcome. Remember my math and science proofs? Similarly, we are told to *prove* the good, acceptable and perfect (or complete) will of God, and to *find out* what pleases Him. In James 1:3, we're told that the *trying*, or proving, of our faith develops, or "works out" endurance.

You might ask, "What's the difference between finding out and proving His will? How can I prove what I don't know?"

I think of a story from my own past, one that always reminds me how faithful God is. When I left the ministry and enrolled in the electrical engineering program, I wasn't sure I was making the right decision. Yes, I had an interest and aptitude for engineering and a strong desire in my heart that I should try to earn a degree in this field. I was also attracted by the substantial starting salary I could expect upon graduation. But there was no clear indication beyond that.

This was a time when many people in my church were relying on haphazard and mystical ways to find God's will, in search of the ever elusive "peace." On top of this, I was sorting through the guilt of leaving the ministry. I asked God again and again to show me His will, but got no direct answer. Although I kept asking Him if I were doing the right thing, I finally decided it was time to make a move, to do *something*. Because I was receiving so much conflicting advice, I went to God and prayed, "Lord, I think this is what you want me to do. I'm going to start down this path. If this isn't what you want, then please stop me." I figured out what was required to enroll and went to the local university and signed up for classes.

God never laid out the whole plan for me. Instead, he opened and closed doors one at a time along the way, giving me confirmations, dead ends, and bits of insight as I moved forward. Once I started school, I felt a strong sense of urgency in my heart that I should complete the degree program in three years. This was an extremely aggressive goal. Most people take four to five years to complete an undergraduate engineering program. Regardless, soon after I started the first semester, I sat down with the university catalog and mapped out a plan for the courses I would have to take in six semesters plus summer school over the next three years. I laid the catalog on my dresser, opened to the pages with the electrical engineering syllabus, and prayed over it every day until I was finished. I offered the whole endeavor before God and said, "Lord, not my will, but yours."

There were many challenges over the next three years. Some were so severe I almost quit—more than once. God was faithful, though, and gave me the strength to make it through each "test" that came along. All the while, the catalog remained opened on my dresser. Whenever I completed a course, I drew a line through the name of the course. I often grew discouraged by how few lines were drawn and how many courses remained to be completed. Over time, I crossed out more and more classes and could at last see my goal within reach. When I finished the program, I finally closed the catalog, lines drawn through all of the course names. I can't begin to tell you how good it felt to get down on my knees and thank God for letting me make it all the way through.

The story didn't end there. I told you earlier about my summer internship with the engineering company in Dallas and the strong desire I had to get my MBA at one of the top universities in the country. I prayed to God to stop me if this wasn't what He wanted me to do. Seeing no closed doors, I applied to six "top twenty" business schools and was accepted to four of them. Now I had to decide which school to attend.

After talking to my family, friends, and church leaders, I finally settled on a prestigious school in the Northeast, one that was more expensive than any of the others. This school appealed to me because it was in a part of the country where I'd never lived before. It had a leading national reputation in managerial finance, the field I intended to study. The school also had a small student body, which would allow more interaction with the professors and other students. It would put me in a good position to find a good job after I graduated. I made plans to attend and tried to line up the money to go.

I had one small problem. I was broke.

My Bible college and electrical engineering courses were paid for by the Vietnam-era G.I. Bill and scholarships from each school. But I didn't have a dime for the MBA program. For about three months, I explored every legal option I could think of, but could not line up any money. It was frustrating, again, to feel like I had been led by God down a certain road only to find a big "dead end" sign parked in front of me.

One day, I got a notice in the mail for the initial tuition payment of $20,000 (in mid-1980s dollars) that was due in two weeks. It was twenty grand more than I had. When I brought this up to several of my Christian friends, they whistled, raised their eyebrows, and said, "How it can be God's will for you to go to that school? You'll never get that kind of money. You should have chosen a cheaper school." Of course, Satan was right there too, Johnny-on-the-spot, accusing and planting his own seeds of doubt. "Tom, you schmuck, you chose this school because of your own pride! You don't deserve to go there! Christians settle for second best, don't you know that?"

I got angry and prayed to God, "Lord, do you really want me to go to this school? If not, why did you let me get accepted? Are you testing my faith or telling me I truly only deserve second best? Do I have to pass up this opportunity?" I got madder and prayed more intensely: "God, is twenty thousand dollars too tall an order for you? Do you really want me to miss out on this opportunity of a lifetime because I can't get the money?"

When I think back on this time, I consider it the breakthrough moment of my Christian experience, my second "come to Jesus" moment with God. I prayed many times throughout each day as the payment deadline approached. Finally, I got to the point where my prayer went like this: "What is this about, Lord? You own the cattle on the thousand hills! Can you come up with this money or not? Show me that you can come through!" The more I prayed, the more I believed that God wanted me at this school. I told Jennifer, my officemate at the engineering company, who was also a Christian, "If I don't get the money this year, I'll try again next year and the next year and the year after that, until I do."

Here I was, like the farmer, wondering "what God does" and "what I do." *Should I wait another year or two and earn the money or is God going to provide it now?* Either way, I decided I'd continue down this path, because I believed it was where He wanted me to go. All the doors were open except this one, and it was now completely up to Him. I felt I'd done everything I could—earned the engineering degree in three years, made good grades, applied to the best schools possible, and went after all the financial aid for which I was eligible. Most importantly, I laid this desire, and my life, on the altar. "God, not my will, but yours. Take away the desire and lead me in another direction if this isn't what you want me to do. Help me to be a good steward of what you have given me."

You know what? I got the money. It came in the form of several student loans, none of which I had applied for prior to this time. God clearly opened some previously slammed shut doors to provide the money. He put some very helpful people, especially Susan, the financial aid director at the school, into my path. She helped me work out some incredibly complex issues in a short time.

Of course, when my friends and fellow church members heard the word "loans," they whistled and rolled their eyes once again, asking, "How are you going to pay back those loans? Doesn't the Bible teach that you shouldn't go into debt? What about the verse that says, 'Owe no man anything'?" I asked God the same questions, with Proverbs 22:7, the verse about the borrower being servant to the lender, ringing loudly in my ears. After all I'd been through, I had to believe these loans were the provisions God had miraculously sent me, so I prepared to go to this school and follow the plan I felt He had laid on my heart.

I also knew there is a difference between *debt* and *leverage*. This was about stewardship, not self-indulgence. I wasn't taking out huge loans to buy a car that would depreciate by ten percent when I drove it off the lot. I wasn't running up credit card debt to buy stuff I would throw away the following year. No, I was taking out these loans so that I could prepare myself for a better-paying job at the other end of the MBA program and go into the business world where I believed God wanted me to be. If I was perhaps doing this to impress anyone else, that took a back seat to my desire to follow His lead. The desire to attend business school came from Him in the first place, I thought, and it was now my obligation to obey no matter how scary it looked. I believed if God had provided these loans, He'd certainly provide the way to pay them off. It was up to me to wait for Him to show me the way at the right time

One afternoon, shortly after I got to the school, I walked around the Quad, the center of the university, and thanked God for the miracle of being there. Two years later, I graduated and landed a job in Southern California. *Finally!* For the first time in years, it looked like the perpetually-closed door to the

West Coast was now open. Here was a great opportunity, but it came with another catch: the salary for this particular job was several thousand dollars a year lower than the offers I had in other parts of the country.

I didn't see how I could pay back the school loans, which would consume over half my take-home pay before rent, gas, food, tithe—everything. I began to worry anew that my friends, and Satan, would be proven correct. Should I have gone to a cheaper school or taken a higher-paying job somewhere else? Just as I'd compared schools, I looked at each of these jobs and felt that the one in California was the best fit for my background, my interests—and my dreams. I claimed that well-known passage, Psalm 37:4–5, "Delight yourself in the Lord and he will give you the desires of your heart. Commit your way to the Lord; trust in him and he will do this." I looked at different ways to save money and pay the school loans, and I asked God to provide a way to honor Him and pay off the debts early.

In answer to my prayer, God stepped in and provided a most creative solution. Shortly after I started my job, I was given the opportunity to take a long-term project assignment in Seattle, where all my living expenses would be paid. Before this time, I wasn't even aware the company did such a thing. *Okay, God, it looks like I'll have to put Southern California on hold a little longer,* I thought. By this time I was learning to trust God and His ways. If it meant spending time in Seattle, well, there must be a reason, if only to pay off the loans early.

I grabbed hold of the opportunity and landed in Seattle in the middle of a big snowstorm. I didn't see the sun for months. For a Texas boy who is used to over three hundred days of sunshine a year, the rainy Pacific Northwest was a huge change. God blessed me with an interesting job and some great coworkers. I learned many things that prepared me for the work I did in the software business over the next twenty years. During the two years in Seattle, God provided enough money to pay off the school loans several years early.

What did I learn from this experience? First, I learned that God doesn't expect us to settle for second best. He does own the cattle on the thousand hills and can summon a bird of prey or a man from a faraway country to work His will. If we're on the altar and surrendered to Him, if God and not something else is on the throne of our hearts, and we feel led to do something bold, we should examine that leading very closely. It's likely from Him. Second, I learned that God rewards bold faith, good stewardship, and submission to His guidance.

When we hear the word "sacrifice," how many of us Christians think it is about giving up something to accept another thing of less value? Listen, we give up ourselves in order to free the God of the Universe to open the floodgates of heaven and rain down His blessings on us. Third, I learned that living by faith is following God when He challenges us with something big. It is holding on to Him with all our might, trusting Him, until He delivers it. It is proving God's will.

THAT I MAY KNOW HIM

I had been saved for over fifteen years when I experienced this breakthrough with God. He powerfully showed His ability to provide my needs while giving me the desires of my heart. More importantly, He gave me a greater blessing: I know Him a lot better now. My view of how God feels about me was forever changed. He cut through many of the things I had been taught by others and showed His true nature to me. As a result of this experience, I have learned that God truly wants His children to be in position to receive His abundant blessings. That position is on the altar, with Him on the throne of our hearts.

God's best for us is better than anything we could desire on our own. Paul made this observation in Philippians 3:7–9, where he said:

> But whatever was to my profit I now consider loss for the sake of Christ.

> What is more, I consider everything a loss compared to the surpassing greatness of knowing Christ Jesus my Lord, for whose sake I have lost all things.

> I consider them rubbish, that I may gain Christ and be found in him, not having a righteousness of my own that comes from the law, but that which is through faith in Christ—the righteousness that comes from God and is by faith.

Compared to knowing God, all of life's trappings and successes pale into insignificance. Earlier in Philippians 3, Paul listed his impeccable Jewish credentials for the benefit of those who had been led astray by the Judaizers, whom he called "dogs" and "mutilators of the flesh." Pretty strong feelings there, wouldn't you say? He used some other interesting terms when he compared his earthly credentials to his relationship with Christ. In their Bible commentaries, John MacArthur and Warren Wiersbe make note of the words "profit" and "loss" used in verses 7 and 8. For the benefit of his audience, Paul was apparently going through his own accounting exercise to show that, compared to a strong, personal, and intimate relationship with Jesus Christ, all of his past accomplishments would end up in the loss column. He considered them "rubbish." The KJV uses the word "dung." According to verse 9, Paul would rely only on the righteousness that comes by faith in Christ.

There is something else to consider here. Warren Wiersbe, in *The Bible Exposition Commentary*, identifies Paul's Roman citizenship as one of the things he counted loss for the sake of Christ. Acts 22:25–30 tells the story of Paul calling on his citizenship to stop a group of Roman soldiers from beating him, to get the attention of the chief captain, and force a hearing between the military leadership and the Jewish council of priests. Paul didn't completely give up his Roman citizenship; he just didn't value it as he had before. He still considered it an instrument to be used as necessary to fulfill his mission.

In Acts 21:24, Paul told the elders of the church at Ephesus that he considered his life worth nothing. He knew he had to go back to Jerusalem and possibly face death at the hands of the Jews. Paul had placed himself on the altar, dying to his own desires so he could live to Christ's. He said his primary goal was to finish the race and complete the mission God had given him. He believed that mission was to testify for the gospel of God's grace—in Jerusalem and then in Rome. Paul's complete surrender enabled God to work freely and accomplish His ultimate plan through him. He could give Paul the most daring and dangerous missions, knowing he would not shy away no matter the personal cost.

In Philippians 3:10–11, Paul went on to tell his readers what it meant for him to know Jesus Christ:

> *I want to know Christ and the power of his resurrection and the fellowship of sharing in his sufferings, becoming like him in his death,*

> *And so, somehow, to attain to the resurrection from the dead.*

Paul wanted to know Christ from experience, not from an intellectual, academic perspective. In Philippians 3:10, he identified the two major characteristics of Christ's own life and mission: the power of His resurrection and the fellowship of His suffering. Obviously, these two characteristics share a vital link. The power of Christ's resurrection is the key to His victory over Satan and the focus of our future with Him in eternity. In Ephesians 1:19–20, Paul said the same power that raised Jesus Christ from the dead is available to us as we live our lives for Him today. He wanted to know this power.

Many people think this power of Christ should be more apparent today, bringing down the works of Satan in a forceful, visible way. But the power of His resurrection works in ways we cannot fathom. Paul, sitting in the Roman jail, knew the power is most effective when God applies it, according to His ultimate plan, to the human heart.

Have you thought about why God has taken so long, according to 1 John 3:8, to "destroy the works of the devil"? Consider this: every day that goes by is another opportunity for another individual to accept God's free gift of salvation in Jesus Christ. Every day is another opportunity for a Christian to lie on the altar and allow God to work His ultimate plan through him or her. Every day is another opportunity for a Christian to persevere, win the prize, and reap the harvest of righteousness and peace. Every day, believers pass from this life to the next, and in the words of Matthew 25:21 and 23, earn the praise of the Lord when He says, "Well done, good and faithful servant. Enter into the joy of the Lord."

Paul understood that the resurrection power was closely tied to the fellowship of His suffering. He reminded his spiritual son Timothy of this in 2 Timothy 1:7–9:

> For God did not give us a spirit of timidity, but a spirit of power, of love and of self-discipline.

So do not be ashamed to testify about our Lord, or ashamed of me his prisoner. But join with me in suffering for the gospel, by the power of God,

Who has saved us and called us to a holy life—not because of anything we have done but because of his own purpose and grace.

Did you notice what he said in verse 8? "Suffering for the gospel by the power of God." Isn't that an interesting paradox? Paul encouraged Timothy to suffer in His strength, not his own weakness. Paul, who had been through so many incredible journeys in his Christian experience, told another group of believers, the Thessalonians, about suffering by the power of God. In 2 Thessalonians 1:3–6 (NLT), he wrote:

Dear brothers and sisters, we can't help but thank God for you, because your faith is flourishing and your love for one another is growing.

We proudly tell God's other churches about your endurance and faithfulness in all the persecutions and hardships you are suffering.

*And God will use this persecution to show his justice and **to make you worthy of his Kingdom** [emphasis mine], for which you are suffering.*

In his justice he will pay back those who persecute you.

To understand Paul's comment "to make you worthy of His Kingdom," let's go back to Philippians 3:10–11. Paul said that he wanted become like Christ in His death (verse 11), "and so, somehow, to attain to the resurrection from the dead." The Greek word Paul used for "resurrection" is *exanastasin*, a word used nowhere else in the Bible. It literally means "out-resurrection," and several commentators believe it may refer to the Rapture of the Church. The phrase "to attain to the resurrection from the dead" literally means "to arrive at the out-resurrection from the dead bodies." As Paul says in 1 Corinthians 15:54, "When the perishable [body] has been clothed with the imperishable, and the mortal with immortality, then the saying that is written will come true: 'Death has been swallowed up in victory.'"

Paul was striving to achieve the full impact of the victory in Christ. He didn't want to just show up in heaven as a beneficiary of Jesus Christ's "fire insurance," but wanted to be ushered into God's Kingdom with a great welcome home for having demonstrated a life of commitment and sacrifice to Him.

This is not about working our way to heaven, or depending on our suffering to save us. This is about steadfastly resisting and overcoming the lies and deceit of the enemy. It is achieving the victory at the end of our race, of obtaining the peaceable fruit of righteousness at the final harvest. It is the reward for a sacrificed life given completely to God. It is the blessing of fulfilling the missions prepared for us by Jesus Christ, who loved us and gave Himself for us.

FOR SUCH A TIME AS THIS

One book of the Old Testament tells a great story about two people who had the willingness to sacrifice and lay down their own will, and the wisdom and character to obey when God gave them a difficult and challenging mission. By doing so, they were used by Him to realize a huge victory over Satan in preserving His people, the Jews, from extermination. This book of the Bible involves a young girl, the girl's cousin, a powerful king, and the king's evil prime minister.

The young girl's name was Hadassah, and we know her today as Esther for the Old Testament book named after her. She was a beautiful Jewish girl who lived near the Persian capital city of Susa, in what is now western Iran. Esther lived in this city a few decades after the Jews had been released by the Persians from Babylonian captivity to return to Jerusalem, about five hundred years before the birth of Christ. The story begins in the third year of the reign of Ahasuerus, King of Persia. Many scholars believe he is Xerxes, the great Persian ruler who invaded Greece and fought against the *triakosioi*, the group of three hundred Spartan warriors who held off tens of thousands of Persian soldiers at the Battle of Thermopylae in 480 BC.

At the time of our story, Xerxes was the most powerful man in the world and was worshipped by many as a god. In the third year of his reign, he held a huge, six-month feast to celebrate his military victories over Babylon and Egypt, and he invited the Queen of Persia to join him at the banquet. Some commentators believe that he wanted her to perform a lewd dance in front of the party-goers. She refused, so Xerxes' ministers passed a law to send her away, and his aides began a search for a new queen. There was a kind of "American Idol" search throughout the Persian Empire for the new queen, and, lo and behold, Esther won the prize.

But there was a problem: her cousin Mordecai, who had raised Esther after her parents died, discovered a plan by the king's prime minister to kill all of the Jews in the Persian Empire. Mordecai told Esther of the plot and asked her to go tell the king. She was afraid to do so. She knew that going to the king without first having an invitation could invite a death sentence. But cousin Mordecai, believing she was the only hope to keep the Jews from being slaughtered, kept up the pressure.

As the story tells us, Esther appeared before the king, uninvited. He was happy to see her and raised his golden scepter toward her. She told him the whole situation, and he became very angry at Haman, the king's prime minister and the ringleader of the plan to kill the Jews. The king sentenced Haman to death by hanging on a set of gallows that had been built to hang Mordecai. The story ends with Esther and Mordecai celebrating a feast with the Jews, who had been delivered from another of Satan's murderous schemes.

Why is Esther's story important to us today? Because she was faithful in performing the mission God gave to her through her cousin Mordecai. She had no idea why she had been picked out of a crowd of beautiful young women to be queen to the most powerful ruler in the world. She did not know what was behind Haman's attack on the Jews. Although she asked Mordecai and the Jews in Susa to fast for three days before she went in to the king, she did not know what would happen. But she did know enough to do the right thing, to respond to God's mission, and to show courage and endurance when she approached the king.

We find another Old Testament story of courageous obedience with Shadrach, Meshach and Abednego in Daniel 2. These three Hebrews refused to bow to the golden image that Nebuchadnezzar, the powerful ruler of Babylon, had set up. As a result, they were placed in a fiery furnace. As you know, the three survived the fire and Nebuchadnezzar put out a decree to honor the God of Israel and promoted Shadrach, Meshach and Abednego to high positions of responsibility in his government.

You may ask, "What does that have to do with me? These are people in the Bible, people God used in specific ways to accomplish His plan."

We've looked at several instances where the Bible says that these stories are for our benefit and instruction. God's Word is the most complete and up-to-date revelation of Himself in our church age, when, as many authors have observed, "heaven is silent." 2 Timothy 3:17, 1 Corinthians 10:11, and Hebrews 1:1–2 reinforce this truth. The Old Testament stories of Esther and the three Hebrews are examples of people who laid themselves on the altar to complete God's missions, no matter the consequences. Let's look at Esther 4:12–14 to see a question Mordecai asked her in the critical moment of trial. It is relevant to us today:

> *When Esther's words were reported to Mordecai, he sent back this answer: "Do not think that because you are in the king's house you alone of all the Jews will escape.*

> *"For if you remain silent at this time, relief and deliverance for the Jews will arise from another place, but you and your father's family will perish. And who knows but that you have come to royal position for such a time as this?"*

"Who knows but that you have come to royal position for such a time as this?" Here, I believe, is a challenge to every Christian who has ever been faced with doing the right thing versus keeping a position of employment, material possessions, a relationship, or even their personal safety. Just as Esther only knew she had been chosen to be Xerxes' queen, we may only know we are in a certain place and confronted with a certain decision with no clue why. God's ultimate will is going to get done one way or another, but He presents us with a unique and specific mission. We will answer for the choice we make in our response.

Consider a vivid example from recent history: the rise of Adolf Hitler in Germany during the 1930s and the effect this geopolitical turn of events would have on a Dutch family who ran a small watch repair business outside

Amsterdam. Hitler, another in the long line of tyrants whom Satan has used to try to destroy God's people and thwart His ultimate plan, took deliberate, step-by-step action to remove the liberties of the Jews. These actions came into the open on November 11, 1938, a horrible night called *Kristallnacht*, or "Night of the Broken Glass," when Nazi thugs and sympathizers smashed the shops and homes of many Jews living in Germany, murdering over ninety of them. That night essentially opened the doors to the "Final Solution," Hitler's plan to exterminate over six million Jews in concentration camps located throughout Germany and Poland. This campaign of genocide is remembered today as the *Shoah*, or Holocaust.

Where was the church in Germany during that time? Several Christians spoke out and paid with their own lives. Most, however, did not. In thousands of ways, they rationalized their unwillingness to get involved. What kind of a stand would you and I have made had we lived there at the time? Would we have done the right thing? Would we have put ourselves on the altar to God as a living sacrifice?

Corrie Ten Boom was a middle-aged Dutch woman who, along with her father and sister, ran their small watch repair shop in Haarlem, a town just outside Amsterdam. She tells her family's story of courage and faithfulness in the book *The Hiding Place*. The name of her book is taken from the small compartment in their house where they hid Jewish refugees from searches by Nazi storm troopers, the Gestapo, and tattletale neighbors.

I was working on an information technology project in Amsterdam one summer in the late 1990s when Kathy and I had the opportunity to visit this house. We wept when we saw the little compartment and realized the extent of Corrie's and her family's sacrifice. None of them had a Bible college education or a "call" to preach in the full-time ministry. They were instead presented with a choice and they paid dearly for it. Her father and sister died at the hands of the Nazis while Corrie survived the brutal horrors of a concentration camp.

Corrie lived into her nineties, leading a bold and fruitful worldwide ministry based on her trials and suffering in the concentration camp. God used her experiences to bring thousands to Jesus Christ. According to her book, Corrie's family was presented with challenges and tests, one after another, step by step, to do the right thing, to which they responded faithfully in submission and obedience to God. How many other Christians living in the same town at the time passed up the opportunity to be used of God in this way?

I think of how Shadrach, Meshach, and Abednego responded to King Nebuchadnezzar, ruler of Babylon, when he arrogantly asked them what god would be able to deliver them from his hand. In Daniel 3:17–18, they replied:

If we are thrown into the blazing furnace, the God we serve is able to save us from it, and he will rescue us from your hand, O king.

But even if he does not, we want you to know, O king, that we will not serve your gods or worship the image of gold you have set up.

You and I may not know why we're in a particular situation where we are confronted with a choice between right and wrong. The choice is between serving the Living God of the Bible or a false idol, and may bring suffering or loss. Nevertheless, as Paul said in Romans 12:1, we're to present our bodies a living sacrifice, and keep in mind, as 1 Samuel 15:22 says, "To obey is better than sacrifice."

THE KEY WORD IS "LIVING"

We may never be given a mission as costly and dangerous as the one God gave to Corrie Ten Boom. But all of us will be called on to perform missions for God that are uniquely tailored to us and are equally important to His ultimate plan. These missions will more often than not take place outside the church walls. Paul encouraged us to be a "living sacrifice," not a dead one. That means we're in the midst of a life-long process, an ongoing activity with lots of give and take, victories and failures, and periods of strength and weakness. We'll have moments of doubt, fear, and uncertainty as we learn to put ourselves on the altar and Him on the throne, following the Lord no matter the consequences. Some of us may even drop out of the race for a while. But God has promised us He's with us every step of the way. He challenges us to not give up on Him or quit for good in discouragement or bitterness. He does not want us to leave Him to follow another god, a false idol.

An inspirational story about King David took place early in his reign when he was in his battle headquarters in the cave of Adullam, fighting against the Philistines. At this time, the Philistine army had captured his hometown of Bethlehem and was garrisoned there. We pick up the story in 2 Samuel 23:15:

> *David longed for water and said, "Oh, that someone would get me a drink of water from the well near the gate of Bethlehem!"*

> *So the three mighty men broke through the Philistine lines, drew water from the well near the gate of Bethlehem and carried it back to David. But he refused to drink it; instead, he poured it out before the Lord.*

Think about it: these men risked their lives to get water for their king, and he wouldn't drink it. Instead, he poured it on the ground as an offering to the Lord. What did this say to his men? To answer that, let's think of another man from Bethlehem: Elimelech, the husband of Naomi, who moved to the land of false gods when there was a famine in Israel. As we saw from the book of Ruth, God judged Elimelech because of his idolatry and lack of faith in Him.

In this case, David made a strong and powerful statement to God and to his army. He said, in effect, "God, you are in charge and we are committed to following you. I trust you to provide my needs. To show my soldiers this is not about me, I will honor you with an offering, brought here through the courage of these brave men." I'm sure David wanted very much to power down that whole flask of water to satisfy his thirst. Because he sacrificed it to the Lord, God honored David by allowing him to defeat his enemies and finally bring peace to Israel.

You might say, "Of course, Tom, that's King David. Certainly he would do something like that. How can I expect to have such faith, or to even know when I'm faced with such a momentous decision as the great saints of the Bible or legendary, courageous Christians like Corrie Ten Boom?" I would respond that we should go back to Paul's desire to *know* the Lord. We can, for example, demonstrate such faith in as simple a circumstance as being tempted to go into a convenience store and buy a lottery ticket because we don't see how we can pay our bills. The choice to resist this temptation is saying to God, "I believe you will take care of my needs. I'll pour the good-tasting water on the ground as an offering to you and drink the nasty stuff here in the cave because I know you're doing a work through me while I'm here." Building a close, intimate relationship with God is the way to gain the faith, courage, and strength to perform the missions He calls us to perform.

What does this intimate relationship look like? The answer may surprise you. In the Psalms, we see many places where David expressed his doubts and fears to the Lord. I don't know about you, but for the longest time I felt like I couldn't be open and honest with God about my own doubts and fears. I was told that expressing doubts to God showed my lack of faith. I was also told to rejoice always and to "count it all joy."

Talk about a no-win situation.

Fortunately, it's not true. David shows us that "rejoicing always" doesn't rule out an honest dialog with God. "Honest dialog" can be translated "screaming match." I rejoice that I'm married to Kathy, but you should hear some of our honest dialog. Open and honest communication is what makes a strong marriage. How much more does it make a strong relationship with our God, the One who sent His own Son to die for us on the cross, the One Who wants us to call Him "Daddy"?

David cried to God in Psalm 61:2, "From the ends of the earth I call to you, I call as my heart grows faint; lead me to the rock that is higher than I." David yelled at God in Psalm 22:1, "My God, my God, why have you forsaken me?" Jesus Christ Himself painfully screamed the same question to His Father from the cross while He was enduring the shame and suffering of that incredible moment in God's ultimate plan.

Rick Warren said something in his bestselling book *The Purpose Driven Life* that made quite an impression on me. He said it's okay to openly express our feelings to God and yell at Him when we're hurt, angry, scared, tired, doubtful, betrayed, whatever. He reminded us that God can take it. The Lord God Almighty is big enough to handle any emotions we might lay before Him during the tough times.

We need to believe God is right and just, and He is worth following with an undivided heart. His plan is perfect in the context of eternity, it's higher than ours, and He will reveal it to us in His own time, according to Romans 8:28, for our good. Romans 5:5 and Ephesians 1:8 tell us He has poured out His love and lavished His grace on us. He loves us so much He sent His Son to die for us and has prepared for us unspeakable riches and glory in His Kingdom.

God expects us to have a real, two-way relationship with Him, and to let Him know how we feel. At the same time, we need to listen to Him, to pay attention to the signals He's giving us through His Word, through wise counsel, through the circumstances we face each day, and through prayer. This is an ongoing thing—while we're talking to God, He's sending messages to us. The closer we get to Him, the better we can understand what He's saying.

PURIFICATION THROUGH SACRIFICE

Even when we know all of this, God may sometimes bring an event into our lives for which we are completely unprepared, a major shock to our system that leaves us profoundly shaken and rudderless. What do we do when our world is rocked to its foundations?

While I was serving in Iraq, the family across the street from Kathy and me lost their twenty-two-year-old son in a car accident with a drunk driver, three days before Christmas.

A friend of mine recently sent me a YouTube video of a young Christian couple whose baby son lived only ninety-nine days before succumbing to multiple congenital birth defects. Their story made me weep, not only for the terrible pain they went through, but for the courage and faith they showed throughout their son's short life and for the honor they gave to the Lord for "letting us have him for a little while. We'll see him again."

I can't think of anything more heartbreaking than losing a child.

James and Grace, a couple of dear friends from the Bible college days, woke up one Sunday morning not too long ago to get ready for church and found their eighteen-year-old son Joey had passed away during the night. No previous health problems, no rebellion or open sin, no warning, no nothing. He was just gone, gone home to be with the Lord. James and Grace were strong enough, and selfless enough, to share their story on Facebook as it unfolded. It was incredible to see so many people responding to them on the website, praying for them, lifting them up, and offering to help.

My friends have drawn significant comfort and encouragement from an event that took place about a year before their son died. Joey and his older brother Ben were football players, and had spent an afternoon going through an exhausting workout. At the end, Ben challenged his younger brother to carry him on his back the length of the football field. You may remember the "death crawl" scene from the movie *Facing the Giants*, where the young team captain, blindfolded and on all fours, carries another player on his back across the football field. The coach yells and encourages him, "Thirty more steps, twenty more steps, ten more steps!" The young captain is in excruciating pain and feels like he can't go on. "Five more steps!" He thinks he's gone fifty yards, but when the coach tells him to take off his blindfold, he sees that he's gone one hundred yards, the entire length of the field.

In the same way, Ben challenged Joey to carry him, shouting the words "ten more yards" to encourage him to continue when Joey's body screamed in pain and fatigue. Ben shared this story at Joey's funeral service, and the response of those who heard it, not only in the service but on Facebook, was overwhelming. James, Grace, their son Ben, and their daughters now use the words "ten more yards" as a memorial to Joey and a challenge to each other.

Their words remind me of David and his three mighty men pouring out their drink offering to God. Despite their excruciating pain and suffering, my friends have made "ten more yards" a pact with the Lord God that they will not quit while there are missions yet to accomplish here on earth. These words are their promise to Joey, their son and brother who is now with the Lord, that they will fight the good fight of the faith and run the race with endurance to the finish line.

As they try to regroup from this time of heart-rending struggle, James and Grace know in their hearts that our years here on earth do not begin to tell the whole story of our existence. We are all on missions for which the purpose may not be revealed to us until we get to eternity. God wants us to die with Christ, to put it all on the altar for Him. For His own purposes, He may take away something near and dear to our hearts to give us the opportunity, like David, to pour it out as an offering to Him.

Those who have passed through this painful crucible come out refined as gold and, as Paul said in 2 Thessalonians 1:5, proving their faith worthy of the Kingdom. They own a perspective few of us can truly appreciate, one that will resonate throughout eternity. My friends James and Grace may never in this life understand why their son was called home to heaven so early and unexpectedly. But they do know God has chosen them for this purpose and is even now opening doors they would never have been able to go through before.

I truly believe that God will, in this life, give to James and Grace and their family the "peaceable fruit of righteousness" that comes through their submission to such a costly sacrifice. I also believe with all my heart that one day you and I will see them reunited with Joey in heaven, standing with the Lord Jesus Christ in blazing gold and white: pure, refined, redeemed, and glorified by the blood of the Lamb of God.

John wrote in Revelation 16:7:

> *And I heard the altar respond: "Yes, Lord God Almighty, true and just are your judgments."*

PART III: PROMISES

I hope these four perspectives of a victorious Christian life will be a source of strength, comfort, and encouragement as you follow God's will for your life. By now you should realize that God's will is about building endurance and accepting the missions He places in front of us. God wants us to be strong, godly, clear-minded, disciplined, and completely submitted to Him. In this last section, I want to share more promises God has made to us as we follow Him on our journey. I pray you will receive as great a blessing in learning about them and putting them into practice as I have.

GLIMPSES OF HIS GLORY

Not too long ago, I read a book on God's will by a well-known pastor/author that was so depressing I had a hard time getting out of bed the next morning. This book focused almost exclusively on the struggles and sufferings we Christians undergo in this life and left it at that. It's almost as if the author had said, "Life's hard. It gets worse. Deal with it."

What a pity! It seemed like he was offering us a cake but serving it in the form of its ingredients and not telling us how to put them together. A pile of sugar and flour here, a couple of broken eggs there, a cup of milk over here, a puddle of melted butter over there. Oh, and let's throw in three hundred degrees of oven heat just to make it more challenging, but hey, there's no purpose to the heat other than to make us hot.

Look, I'm not one to enjoy living a life of all seriousness, pain, and suffering. I love to have fun—I was voted "Class Clown" in college. But, over the course of the past thirty-five years, I've seen that God works in serious and challenging ways for a reason. As we saw in the "Christian as farmer" perspective, He gives each of us a unique set of basic ingredients, seeds if you will, called the talents, gifts, and circumstances of our lives. He's given us the process, called unique missions or projects, through which we work with these ingredients and cultivate them to generate the peaceable fruit of righteousness. He conditions us, as Peter explained in his "strength training program for godliness," to partake in His holiness and meet Him in His full glory.

Even so, why doesn't God show Himself to us once in a while, the way He really is? Why all of the indirect hints, clues, patterns, symbols, and parables in Scripture? Why all the rabbit trails and blind alleys in life? The simple answer is this: if God showed Himself to us as He is, it would kill us!

When I was in Bible college, I took a class that introduced a subject called "Biblical Theology," the study of God's progressive revelation to the human race throughout history. According to this view, we know more about God today than Abraham, Moses, David, Elijah, or even Paul knew. It says God uses the patterns in the Bible to teach us lessons and prepare us for a future with Him. The hints and clues point to His future plans. Peter talks about this in 1 Peter 1:10–12:

> *Concerning this salvation, the prophets, who spoke of the grace that was to come to you, searched intently and with the greatest care,*

> *Trying to find out the time and circumstances to which the Spirit of Christ in them was pointing when he predicted the sufferings of Christ and the glories that would follow.*

> *It was revealed to them that they were not serving themselves but you, when they spoke of the things that have now been told you by those who have preached the gospel to you by the Holy Spirit sent from heaven. Even angels long to look into these things.*

God limits the way He reveals Himself to these glimpses that make up "teaching lessons" to help us better understand our place in His ultimate plan. Here's one powerful example: in Exodus 33: Moses asked to see God's glory, and was told no. God told him to hide in the cleft of a rock on Mount Sinai so he could see only the aftereffects of His full glory as He passed by. Moses was incredibly transformed by the experience. For the rest of his life, he had to walk around with his face covered because it had become so radiant. This incident was recorded and passed down to generations of Jews who realized the importance of Moses meeting God on that mountain.

Centuries later, in 1 Kings 19, the prophet Elijah had run the entire length of Israel to escape the evil queen Jezebel when she threatened to kill him after he had eliminated the prophets of the false god Baal. Elijah was so discouraged by this turn of events, and his long north-to-south escape, that he sat down under a tree in the middle of the desert and asked God to end his life. "I'm tired, Lord, I can't deal with it anymore, take me home. End my life now."

How many of us have prayed something similar? I'm reminded of George Bailey, standing on the bridge just before Clarence Oddbody, AS-2, jumps into the river.

An angel appeared to Elijah in the desert, provided some food and water, and told him to head further south to Mount Sinai, near Egypt. This was the "Mount of God," the same place where Moses hid in the cleft of the rock to see God pass by. When Elijah got there, he hid in a cave. The Bible says in 1 Kings 19:9 that "the Word of the Lord came to him and asked, 'What are you doing here, Elijah?'" Didn't we just read that an angel had led him there? It was obviously a rhetorical question, setting up another teaching lesson. Elijah told the Lord that Israel had broken its covenant with God and killed all of His prophets, and he was the only one left.

In verse 11, He told Elijah to stand on the mountain, and "the Lord passed by," the same thing that happened to Moses in that very spot. But here, in 1 Kings 19, the Lord sent a huge wind that shattered the rocks around Elijah, followed by a big earthquake and a raging fire. The Bible says that the Lord was not in any of these cataclysmic events that, had they happened today, would have made CNN headline news. Instead, after the intense fire, Elijah heard what the KJV calls "a still small voice."

Hiding in the back of the cave to protect himself from God's awesome display of power, he had to walk out to the entrance to hear the whispering voice. I can imagine God whispering his question to Elijah like you or I might ask a child:

What are you doing here, little one?

Elijah said again that he was the only one left in Israel who had remained faithful to God. God replied to him [my paraphrase of 1 Kings 19:15–19 and 2 Kings 2:1, 11]:

> No, Elijah, I've got seven thousand others who haven't worshipped Baal. You're not alone, and now I've got another job for you. Go back the way you came, back to the desert near Damascus, and select the next kings of Syria and Israel. Then choose Elisha to take your place as prophet.
>
> Oh, and one more thing: I'm not going to answer the prayer you asked when you were sitting under the juniper tree in the desert. You're not going to die. You're coming home with me in a chariot of fire!

The story continues in Matthew 17, as well as Mark 9 and Luke 9, on the Mount of Transfiguration. Moses and Elijah appeared and met with Jesus, who was transfigured into a glorified form. Now, why those two? For one, they were the only two from the Old Testament who'd seen Him this way before. Obviously there was a God-given pattern here. Most commentators believe Moses represented the law and Elijah the prophets, which together formed the authoritative Old Testament revelation of Himself that God gave to the nation of Israel. Jesus said in Matthew 5:17 that He came not to abolish the law and prophets, but to fulfill them. In Luke 9:31, Jesus, Moses, and Elijah "spoke about his departure, which he was about to bring to fulfillment at Jerusalem."

Peter, James, and John, standing with Jesus on the mountain, somehow recognized Moses and Elijah. Thinking they had come to usher in the Kingdom of God, Peter asked Jesus if he could set up three tents to celebrate the Feast of Tabernacles. This was an annual event in which the Jews remembered their historical entry into the Promised Land and looked forward to the future Kingdom by living in tents for a week. Mark and Luke made the observation that Peter didn't know what he was saying. Apparently he forgot what Jesus had told them only days earlier, in Luke 9:22: He would go to Jerusalem and be killed. About this time, a voice rang out from heaven telling them to listen to Jesus, the Son of God. Peter, James, and John fell on their faces in terror, as if they were dead. Jesus, alone now, reached down and said, "Gentlemen, get up. Don't be afraid."

Jesus had already revealed His plan to die in Jerusalem, but Peter somehow missed the connection. He certainly understood the reason many years later, though, when he was writing his second letter. Just after he described God's "strength training program of godliness," he recalled his own experience on the Mount of Transfiguration, in 2 Peter 1:16–19:

> *We did not follow cleverly invented stories when we told you about the power and coming of our Lord Jesus Christ, but we were eyewitnesses of his majesty.*
>
> *For he received honor and glory from God the Father when the voice came to him from the Majestic Glory, saying, "This is my Son, whom I love; with him I am well pleased."*
>
> *We ourselves heard this voice that came from heaven when we were with him on the sacred mountain.*
>
> *And we have the word of the prophets made more certain, and you will do well to pay attention to it, as to a light shining in a dark place, until the day dawns and the morning star rises in your hearts.*

God knew Peter would one day be in a position to encourage new believers who were scattered throughout the Roman Empire and under persecution, pointing them to the hope of their future in God's ultimate plan. This plan has patterns that were revealed in part to Moses, Elijah, Peter, James, and John. Peter's personal experience of seeing the glorified Jesus Christ, God's revelation in living form, formed one of those patterns. It also formed his desire to be the right instrument, in the right place and at the right time, to accomplish his missions in God's ultimate plan.

In Revelation 1, the glorified Jesus Christ appeared to John, the elderly apostle living in exile on the island of Patmos outside the harbor of Ephesus. What happened next? The same thing: John, the disciple whom Jesus loved, fell down at Christ's feet as if he were dead. Then what? The Lord Jesus Christ did the same thing He did on the Mount of Transfiguration. Revelation 1:17–19 tells us He laid His hand on John's shoulder and said, "Do not be afraid. I am the First and the Last. I am the Living One; I was dead, and behold I am alive for ever and ever! Write, therefore, what you have seen, what is now and what will take place later."

real *poiema*, His workmanship of Ephesians 2:10. Not a cheap prize, but a reward of eternal value brought about through those missions of good works He chose for us before the foundation of the world.

I remember a quote from one of my favorite Bible college professors:

Sow a thought, reap an act.

Sow an act, reap a habit.

Sow a habit, reap a character.

Sow a character, reap a destiny.

Our character is the proof that our faith is genuine, developed through the trials and sufferings of God's strength-training program. Our destiny is the realization of the hope we have in Jesus Christ of a future Kingdom and eternal fellowship with Him. Our hope, should we endure to the end and overcome, is that we will be rewarded in praise, glory and honor when we stand before our Lord. Paul told us in Romans 5:5 that our hope does not disappoint, and will not fail our expectations.

We can be assured, by the Word of God that abides forever, that we will not be disappointed if we follow these principles of God's will. Titus 1:1-2 says, "for the faith of God's elect and the knowledge of the truth that leads to godliness—a faith and knowledge resting on the hope of eternal life, which God, who does not lie, promised before the beginning of time."

He will make it happen.

As we continue on our journey, and until we behold the lights of that eternal city, the glory of our heavenly home, may we submit to God's strength-training program for godliness. May we, as Paul said, "Endure hardness as a good soldier of the Lord Jesus Christ." May we run according to the rules and win the victor's crown. May we be the first to enjoy the harvest of the peaceable fruit of righteousness. May we, like David, lay down our bodies and our most valued possessions as an offering to the Lord.

May we embrace these four perspectives as "God's will for the rest of us" and live each day to glorify Him!

For updates and additional information, please visit my website: www.godzwill4us.com

Made in the USA
Lexington, KY
21 December 2010